The Stolen Billions: How Gaza's Gas Fields Fuel A Hidden War

GEW Social Sciences Group, Preface by Dr Hichem Karoui

Global East-West (London)

Copyright © 2025 by GEW Social Sciences Group

Preface by Dr Hichem Karoui.

Collection: The Mediterranean Notebooks. Geopolitics.

All rights reserved.

No portion of this book may be reproduced in any form without written permission from the publisher or author, except as permitted by copyright law.

Contents

Gaza: The Hidden War For Resources — 1

1. Introduction: Trump's Plan For Peace — 11
2. The Veiled Conflict — 27
3. Discovery and Promise — 47
4. Economics of Denial — 63
5. Maritime Rights Under Siege — 79
6. Israel's Toolbox of Obstruction — 95
7. The 2023 Heist — 113
8. Trump's Riviera Dream — 131
9. Netanyahu's Echo — 149
10. The Mediterranean Bonanza — 167
11. Toward Justice — 185

Gaza: The Hidden War For Resources
Preface by Hichem Karoui

The sector's untapped gas reserves and the geopolitics of displacement

Security concerns, the fight against terrorism, or long-standing regional conflicts often frame the current destruction in Gaza. In reality, beneath the surface of this conflict lies a less publicised but equally important dimension: the struggle for control of significant offshore natural gas reserves that could change the Palestinian economic outlook – or enrich those who prevent their exploitation. [1] One of the most striking statements in this regard came from Alain Juillet, former director of the General Directorate for External Security (DGSE), who claimed that Gaza's offshore gas fields could generate $3 billion in revenue a year, highlighting an important aspect of the conflict that is often overlooked in mainstream discourse. [2]

The Gaza Marine gas field [3], discovered in 2000 about 36 kilometres off the coast of Gaza, represents more than just an energy resource: it symbolises Palestinian economic sovereignty, which has been systematically denied for 77 years. With reserves estimated at between 1 and 1.4 trillion cubic feet of natural gas (approximately 30 to 35 billion cubic metres), the field could generate between $3 billion and $4 billion in total revenue, providing the legitimate Palestinian Authority (or the existing state) with significant annual revenue for an as yet undetermined period. [4]

The economics of denial

To understand the significance of these figures, it is necessary to put them into context. While Gaza's offshore reserves are modest compared to those of the gigantic Leviathan field (600 billion cubic metres), controlled by Israel, or the Egyptian Zohr field (850 billion cubic metres), their economic impact on Gaza will be transformative. [5] The Leviathan field alone generates approximately $10 billion per year in export revenues, with Israel expected to collect between $57 billion and $74 billion in gas-related taxes over the next decade. [6] For the impoverished Gaza Strip, even a small portion of these revenues would represent economic liberation.

According to the 2019 report by UNCTAD [7] (United Nations Conference on Trade and Development), Palestinians have already lost approximately $2.57 billion due to the ban on exploiting their maritime resources since 2000. [8] This figure increases significantly each year and represents not only a financial loss but also a systematic deprivation of economic development and energy independence, which are the foundations on which the future Palestinian state should be built.

International law and maritime rights

Under the United Nations Convention on the Law of the Sea (UNCLOS), to which Palestine acceded in 2015, the Palestinian state enjoys sovereign rights over its maritime areas, including the exclusive economic zone extending up to 200 nautical miles from its baseline. [9] Palestine officially declared its maritime borders in 2019, with Gaza Marine located within Palestinian territorial waters.

However, Israel, although not a party to the UN Convention on the Law of the Sea, has systematically impeded the development of Gaza Marine by various means [10]: military occupation, restrictions related to the maritime blockade, political obstruction, and, more recently, the granting of gas exploration licenses to international companies in areas within Palestinian maritime borders. [11]

In October 2023, a few days after intensifying its attacks on Gaza, Israel granted licenses to six Israeli and international companies, including Italy's Eni, Britain's BP, and Dana Petroleum, to explore gas in Zone G, 62% of which lies within the maritime borders declared by Palestine. [12]

This constitutes what international legal experts describe as 'plundering' of Palestinian natural resources [13], in violation of Article 55 of the Fourth Geneva Convention of the Hague Code, which prohibits occupying forces from exploiting limited non-renewable resources for commercial purposes.

Trump's vision and Netanyahu's agreement

The various proposals put forward by President Trump regarding Gaza throughout 2025 reveal the extent of the resources behind the humanitarian rhetoric. [14] In February 2025, Trump proposed that the United States 'control' Gaza, with the permanent resettlement of Palestinians in neighbouring countries – a plan he later described as transforming Gaza into the 'Riviera of the Middle East'. [15] While administration officials later backtracked on these statements, claiming that any displacement would be 'temporary', Trump repeatedly returned to the theme of cleaning up Gaza for redevelopment. [16]

Prime Minister Netanyahu's enthusiastic support for Trump's proposals becomes more understandable when viewed through the lens of resource control. [17] Far-right Israeli ministers Bezalel Smotrich and Itamar Ben-Gvir have openly called for the 'voluntary' resettlement (elsewhere) of 2.1 million Palestinians from Gaza and the creation of Israeli settlements in Gaza, policies that international legal experts describe as ethnic cleansing. Smotrich has stated that Gaza is 'an integral part' of Israel and has outlined plans to completely destroy it, with its inhabitants being "concentrated" in the south before leaving 'in large numbers to third countries'. [18]

Trump's '20-point peace plan' presented in September 2025, although more diplomatically worded, contains provisions from Trump's 'economic development plan' that call for the creation of special economic zones, new colonial mechanisms that could facilitate the exploitation of resources by foreigners without the consent or effective control of Palestinians.

Resource context

The vast Mediterranean basin contains approximately 122 trillion cubic feet of natural gas and 1.7 billion barrels of oil, making it one of the world's most important regions in terms of hydrocarbons. [19] Israel's control over Palestinian resources extends beyond the Gaza Strip to include the Majd oil and gas field, located beneath the West Bank, which is estimated to be worth between $84 billion and $120 billion – resources to which Palestinians have no access due to the Israeli occupation. [20]

This systematic deprivation occurs while Israel develops the maritime deposits it controls with impunity, exports billions of dollars' worth of gas to Egypt and Jordan each year, and grants exploration licences in disputed waters. The hypocrisy here is obvious: Israel invokes security reasons to prevent the exploitation of Palestinian gas for the benefit of the Palestinian people while exploiting platforms off the coast of Gaza and running pipelines through Palestinian territorial waters.

Should we believe that Israel has good intentions?

The scale of the resources provides disturbing clarity for

those who believe in Trump's 'good intentions' or consider that Israeli policies in Gaza are motivated purely by security concerns. When political leaders propose to expel the entire indigenous population from a territory rich in energy resources estimated to be worth billions of dollars, when they prevent the exploitation of these resources for 25 years while developing neighbouring fields for their own benefit, and when they grant exploration licences in occupied waters to international companies,

These are not the actions of parties seeking peace and peaceful coexistence. Alain Juillet observes that the profitability of Gaza's gas 'explains the interest in expelling Palestinians from the enclave,' and this is not a conspiracy theory, but a geopolitical reality based on documented policies, violations of law, and economic data.

The picture is clear enough: systematic denial of Palestinian rights to resources, proposals to displace the population, and plans to 'redevelop' Gaza under 'international' or Israeli control.

As energy expert Michael Baron has pointed out, international recognition of the Palestinian state could strengthen legal claims to Gaza's maritime zone. [21] However, Israel and its allies oppose precisely this recognition, as it would establish undeniable sovereign rights over these resources. The war against Gaza is certainly about political control, but it is also undoubtedly about who will profit from the natural resources beneath its waters.

Hichem Karoui, Visiting Researcher at the China-Arab Research Center on Reform and Development of Shanghai International Studies University (SISU).
November 2025.

***

[1] Betsey Piette, Behind Israel's 'end game' for Gaza: Theft of offshore gas reserves. Workers World, 14 November 2023. https://www.workers.org/2023/11/74864/

[2] What future for Gaza? An unsustainable geopolitical impasse. Interview with Alain Juillet by Claude Medori. Open Box TV. https://youtu.be/vAKTsftkNxQ?si=arPz7kURFr4eMfj0&t=1

See also:

J.L. Hardy. The genocide in Gaza represents an annual income of $3 billion for Israel. Le Club Mediapart, 1 July 2024: https://blogs.mediapart.fr/jean-lucien-hardy/blog/010724/le-genocide-de-gaza-represente-un-revenu-annuel-de-3-milliards-de-dollars-pour-israel

Emilien Lacombe. Oil and gas off the coast of Gaza. IDJ, news of the day. 6 February 2025.

https://infodujour.fr/societe/geopolitique/75581-du-petrole-et-du-gaz-au-large-de-gaza

[3] Gaza Marine. CC Energy. https://www.ccenergyltd.com/operations/palestine/overview

[4] Abdrabou A. H. Alanzi, Gaza Marine Gas: Economic Opportunities & Political Challenges in Israeli-Palestinian Conflict. Journals of Business & Management Studies

Vol. 1: Issue 1. 23 June 2025.

https://www.dmjr-journals.com/assets/article/1750629

[5] How much Gas Reserves does Gaza have and who could profit. Sarajevo Times. 23 February 2025. https://sarajevotimes.com/how-much-gas-reserves-does-gaza-have-and-who-could-profit/

[6] Sharon Wrobel, Israel expected to earn up to £74 billion in taxes from natural gas over next decade. The Times of Israel, 30 June 2025. https://www.timesofisrael.com/liveblog_entry/israel-expected-to-earn-up-to-74-billion-in-taxes-from-natural-gas-over-next-decade/

[7] The Economic Costs of the Israeli Occupation for the Palestinian People: The Unrealised Oil and Natural Gas Potential. UNCTAD Report. 2019. https://unctad.org/system/files/official-document/gdsapp2019d1_en.pdf

[8] Patrick Mazza, How is Gaza Offshore Gas Development Tied to the Israeli Invasion?

26 January 2024.

https://www.counterpunch.org/2024/01/26/how-is-gaza-offshore-gas-development-tied-to-the-israeli-invasion/

[9] Rene Lefeber, International Law and the Use of Maritime Hydrocarbon Resources. CIEP/IGU, 2015. https://www.ifri.org/sites/default/files/migrated_files/documents/atoms/files/law_of_the_sea_tf3_igu_final_may_2015.pdf

[10] Qafisheh MM, Bastaki J, Kattan V. Gaza Marine: The facts and the law. Leiden Journal of International Law. 2025;38(1):42-57. doi:10.1017/S0922156525100423

[11] As war rages, Gaza's £4 billion gas field remains untapped. Y net. 20.07.25. https://www.ynetnews.com/environment/article/syfvy39ugl

[12] Murat Temizer, Israel grants gas exploration licence in areas considered to be within Palestine's maritime boundary. Anadolu Agency, 15.02.2024. https://www.aa.com.tr/en/middle-east/israel-grants-gas-exploration-license-in-areas-considered-to-be-within-palestines-maritime-boundary/3138367

[13] Israeli Gas Exploration Licences in Palestine's Maritime Areas Are Illegal and Violate International Law. Al-Haq. 8 February 2024. https://www.alhaq.org/advocacy/22619.html

[14] The Other Reason Trump Wants Gaza: Getting Its Off-Shore Gas. WorldCrunch. 12 February 2025. https://worldcrunch.com/focus/israel-palestine-war/trump-gaza-gas/

[15] Kanishka Singh, Timeline of Trump's remarks on Palestinian displacement, Gaza takeover. Reuters, 8 July 2025. https://www.reuters.com/world/middle-east/trumps-remarks-plan-take-over-gaza-displace-palestinians-2025-02-20/

[16] Amr Hamzawy, Trump's Gaza Peace Plan: Comprehensive, Ambitious, and Uncomfortably Ambiguous. Carnegie Endowment for International Peace. 1 October 2025. https://carnegieendowment.org/emissary/2025/10/gaza-trump-peace-plan-comprehensive-obstacles?lang=en

[17] Franco Ordoñez, Trump announces an agreement with Israel to end war in Gaza. NPR. 29 September

2025. https://www.npr.org/2025/09/29/nx-s1-5556916/trump-israel-gaza-netanyahu

[18] Tinshui Yeung, Trump says Israel will hand over Gaza to US after fighting ends. BBC, 6 February 2025. https://www.bbc.com/news/articles/c4g9xgj2429o

[19] Assessment of Undiscovered Oil and Gas Resources of the Levant Basin Province, Eastern Mediterranean. U.S. Geological Survey. Fact Sheet 2010-3014. March 2010. https://pubs.usgs.gov/fs/2010/3014/pdf/FS10-3014.pdf

[20] Ramon Lopez, Offshore Gaza: gas in deep-water sedimentary reservoir rocks as another element in the conflict. EGU Blogs, 1 December 2023. https://blogs.egu.eu/divisions/ssp/2023/12/01/offshore-gaza-gas-in-deep-water-sedimentary-reservoir-rocks-as-another-element-in-the-conflict/

[21] Recognised, independent Palestinian state could unlock disputed gas wealth, expert says. Arab News. 20 July 2025. https://www.arabnews.com/node/2608797/middle-east

1
Introduction: Trump's Plan For Peace

How Could It Be a Solution Without Ending Israeli Occupation?

Optimism, pessimism and controversy have accompanied the proposed peace plan by the US President Donald Trump, which has been "in the works" for some time. This section of the book aims to situate the plan's main components and delineate them for the reader, and is therefore a preparatory step for the more enduring assessment to follow. We seek to render the strategy and its probable outcomes comprehensively, while still maintaining equity and balance.

The social and political components, demographic and other geopolitical factors of the plan will be scrutinised to enable the reader to grasp its major concepts. Acquiring optimism or scepticism regarding Trump's visions, plans, and constructs, whilst evaluating their feasibility and value, requires the assumption of an open mindset. Readers will be invited on an analytical journey to secure the pertinent information on how the plan aspires to achieve its aims, its objectives, and associated flaws. The subsequent chapters will present the historical, legal, and geopolitical constructs aligned with the plan so that we can apply the dual processes of comprehension and criticism to determine the extent and the limits of its practical utility in fostering enduring peace in the region.

Historical Context of the Conflict

The geopolitics of the Israeli-Palestinian conflict rests on a complicated historical tapestry woven over centuries. Any understanding of the conflict requires examining its history, which is vital for understanding the complexity of factors that have made the dispute so enduring.

The beginnings of the conflict can be traced to the late 19th century, with the spikes of the Zionist movement and the subsequent arrival of Jewish immigrants into the area that was then under the Ottoman Empire. The initial steps of the Zionist pioneers to secure a homeland in what is known as Palestine set in motion the nationalistic tensions between Jews and Arabs, which gave rise to fierce debates over land and sovereignty.

The period following World War I included the collapse of the Ottoman Empire and the beginning of British control of Palestine. This period was a turning point in the history of the conflict. The Balfour Declaration in 1917 allocated the Jewish settlement in Palestine and promised a 'homeland' to the Jews. This greatly increased the conflict between the local Arab population and the new Jewish settlements.

The conflict after World War II was also dreadful. This was a result of the United Nations Partition Plan for Palestine in 1947, which aimed to create a Jewish and Arab state within the Palestine territory. The proposals for the partition of Palestine and the subsequent Arab hostility culminated in the 1948 Arab-Israeli War. This led to the declaration of the State of Israel. Many Arab and Palestinian people became displaced, subject to the ravages of the war.

Subsequent military engagements include the Six-Day War and the Yom Kippur War, and both of these, in conjunction, shifted the political and territorial condition of the region. This also exposed the animosities between the people in the conflict. The violent hostility against the Palestinians, which has continued until today, has violated their borders and expanded the settlement region. This has broadened the conflict even further and deepened the issues.

The Israeli-Palestinian conflict revolves around competing lines of histories, grievances, claims to land, and heritage. It remains intertwined with several historical events and cultural identities. This continues to affect the quest for peace and reconciliation.

The Israeli-Palestinian conflict is one of the most complex. It is layered with political, economic, social, and security complications. All of which the 'Blueprint for Peace' approaches. It is one of the most synthesised attempts towards achieving sustained peace, security, and economic prosperity for all involved parties in the conflict.

Blueprint for Peace – An Overview

The 'Blueprint for Peace' aims to resolve the historical animosities and align cooperative endeavours between the two parties. It does so via in-depth diplomacy, economic and security provision, and cooperation. There seeks to be a controlled and balanced underlying structure for coexistence. Conflict and aspirations from both parties must also be addressed. It is the essence of the 'Blueprint for Peace'.

Also, the Blueprint for Peace utilises the influence and resources of primary global stakeholders for dialogues and trust-building to facilitate and implement vital actions for the advancement of the international setting. Regional, international, and powerful global actors have to be on board to consolidate efforts toward peace and stability in the region.

The balance of the overview is the recognition that the

attainment of peace requires the fulfilment of the rights and interests of all the parties involved, along with the consideration of the underlying geopolitical dynamics. Therefore, the Blueprint for Peace recognises the necessity for the integration of historical grievances, modern-day realities, and future expectations. It recognises the intricacies of the conflict and the essence of identity, citizenship, and bodily integrity to provide a comprehensive view of the multi-layered aspects of the conflict.

The Blueprint for Peace has gathered great potential visions and roles. It goes beyond conventional frameworks and seeks new ways of achieving old goals. It fulfils its ambitious character through its all-encompassing approach to one of the most complex disputes of our era. It has set out to shape the future act of justice by resolving the conflict with the care it deserves. The plan also works as a guide for achieving the outlined goals and serves as a glimmer of hope to those who wish to see durable peace and stability in the region.

Blueprint for Peace: An Overview

The Blueprint for Peace is a well-thought-out document aimed at resolving the Israeli-Palestinian conflict. It sets out an approach to peace that is secure and prosperous for all stakeholders. Apart from peace, the approach includes the political, economic, security, and social aspects of the conflict, all of which are a significant part of the region's interrelated complexities.

The Blueprint for Peace strives to resolve core issues and promote inter-cooperation "for the benefit of both parties".

It is an integrated strategy that uses diplomacy, economic assistance, and military cooperation to build the conditions for stability and the peaceful coexistence of the parties. It hopes to resolve the fundamental issues of the conflict to balance the aspirations of both parties, leaving a fair and lasting solution.

The Blueprint for Peace relies on the global community for the achievement of its goals, which underlines the importance of international collaboration and assistance, as emphasised in the document. It brings the drivers and resources of major global players to the table to facilitate conversations, establish confidence, and take critical actions to pave the way for the advancement of the core-focused activities. This involves working with local stakeholders, global stakeholders, international systems, and power brokers to build a coalition for the achievement of peace and stability in the region.

The most important aspect in this case is the understanding that peace is attained only after considering the rights and interests of all and the prevailing international situation, which is complex. For this reason, the Blueprint for Peace argues that the historical and current grievances and the prospects for the conflict in the future are all highly sensitive and must be controlled. It understands the dynamic and innovative intricacies of self-identity, self-determination, and public order capture. It appreciates the conflict and the various complexities that are associated with it.

The fulfilment of the blueprint for peace transcends the conventional scope of such phenomena while providing new paradigms for age-old challenges. The scope of the blueprint singularly focuses on the aims of the protracted peace conflict. This underlines the seriousness of the blueprint in delivering on the principles of justice, dignity and prosperity, while also fulfilling the aspirations of a myriad of people. The meticulous detailing of the procedures for attaining the goals also makes the plan a mainstay for the people whose aspirations centre on peace and stability within the region.

Occupation and Its Legal Dimensions

Territorial occupation has been a critical factor in the ongoing conflict between Israel and Palestine. Analysing the occupation from a legal viewpoint reveals how complex and intertwined the issue becomes with international law, particularly the Fourth Geneva Convention of 1949. The convention grants certain protections to belligerents' civilian populations and prohibits the controlling state from transferring segments of its own civilian population into any area that it occupies, which, in this case, would be Israel. The discussion surrounding the Israeli occupation, however, remains extremely contentious regarding its practical enforcement. The rights of the Palestinian people continue to be violated in the international arena, with dislocation and the establishment of the Israeli settlements in Palestinian territory being the most pronounced of these, as well as the most flagrant breaches of international law.

In addition, many United Nations Security Council resolutions regarding the Israeli occupation have been issued that, in most cases, question its continuance. UNSC Resolutions 242 and 338 stand out because they emphasise the 'inability of obtaining a territory by warfare' and, in addition, mandate the retreat of the Israeli armed forces from the territories under its occupation. These resolutions set the ground for the position of the rest of the world regarding the Israeli occupation.

It has been legally accepted since the advisory opinion issued by the International Court of Justice (ICJ) in 2004 that the separation barrier constructed by Israel on the occupied Palestinian territories is illegal and contrary to international law. The Court confirmed that the construction of the barrier is illegal and restated the need for Israel to cease the construction of the barrier, dismantle the portions constructed, and pay reparations for the damages. Nevertheless, the barrier still affects the everyday life of Palestinians, and the construction of Israeli settlements does not seem to cease. Beyond the specific legal tools and decisions, the particular context of the occupation has repercussions for the exercise of the right to self-determination of the Palestinian people. The legal limitations of self-determination, which is in and of itself a denial of a fundamental right, result in significant legal issues of the occupation that concern the question of statehood, territorial integrity, and the attainment of self-determination within the international legal order of the Palestinian people. This has made it essential to study the legal aspects of the occupation to grasp the intricate details of the Israeli-Palestinian conflict and the search for durable peace.

Geopolitical Motivations Behind the Plan

The puppeteers behind complexities, vast history, and flowing culture draping from one civilisation to another must first tamper with one of the builders of civilisation – peace – and which civilisation is present within the raging ocean of warfare and within bullies and fragile at-peace Saudi and Iran? The ultimate goal is to capture the big fish from the swamp. The goal is to connect, strengthen, and foster allies, working in unison to counter both internal and regional threats. With plans for peace, the signature style outlines control and subdues rivalry in the region. The Middle East, a strategically placed pearl on the resources necklace, glints and shadows from the hands of the United States, Russia, and China, spanning power. All puppeteers are clenching a thread at the centre of the board, and from above the stream, peace and stealth slant their smokes while portraying strength. The scope is far from limited within; the inner conflicts stretch far past horizons.

In addition, historical warfare and diplomacy—especially praising and demonising one's enemies— influence the geopolitical strategies behind the plan. The decades-long geopolitical attention, intervention, and often direct conflict have produced a tangled framework of relationships that remain fluid and active. These factors do describe elements of frameworks that have grown over decades, and they do converge. Each actor, however, attempts to exploit a particular situation to enhance their respective standing and primary objectives.

The consequences of the plan's geopolitical objectives are equally important, particularly regarding their impact on the overall stability of the region. The Middle Eastern region is interdependent, and, therefore, any attempt to establish peace in that region has consequences that go beyond the direct negotiators. The geopolitical positioning becomes complex due to the involvement of the direct and immediate parties of the conflict, adjoining states, regional groupings, and the global community.

Finally, the goal of a flourishing and peaceful Middle East stands as the motivation for the vision. The plan seeks to resolve the Israeli-Palestinian conflict as a first step to enabling greater collaboration at the regional level and to fostering economic and social development in the area. This dream has strategic components as well; the Middle East in optimal order, stable and prosperous, is a benefit for all the stakeholders of the peace plan. This collection of complex strategic factors is important for understanding the context of the peace proposal and its possible impact on the region.

The Voices of Critics– Lagging Solutions

Every stakeholder involved in providing a blueprint for peace in the Israeli-Palestinian conflict bases their underlying perspectives on the criticisms presented. It is the critical voices that raise the issues with the positive narratives of the almost utopian peace plans. The complexity of the critical voices is a necessary counterweight to the optimistic – sometimes wishful —narrative of peace plans. The most frequent criticisms of peace plans, including those associated with the Trump administration, are those of land and territorial, sovereign, and security, along with the bigger picture of the conflict's fundamental and long-term resolution. They argue, along with many others, that the absence of addressing the fundamental power and inequality relations within any proposed blueprint is a flaw. Additionally, some critics argue that the proposed blueprint fails to consult key stakeholders, particularly the Palestinian leadership, which undermines the blueprint's scope, integrity, and commitment to being holistic and enduring. Furthermore, criticisms also emphasise the lack of fundamental resolutions regarding the Israeli settlements within the occupied territories, which is indeed a vital obstacle.

Moreover, the rights and aspirations of Palestinian refugees, and the ways in which they have been unaddressed, evidently highlight another humanitarian and displacement crisis that originated because of the conflict, which has also been a subject of criticism. Critics also point out the lack of consideration for the wider geopolitical consequences and ramifications of endorsing a plan that significantly lacks regional context and ignores international legal concerns. As such, the underlying logic of any purported peace plan and its enforceability will remain precariously intertwined and dependent upon international law and treaties, as well as the interests of neighbouring countries in participating and cooperating in the peace process. In particular, these criticisms suggest a need for an approach that is likely to rectify historical wrongs and non-principled violations of human rights, such as genuine mutual recognition and respect. This extensive criticism highlights the gaps in the effectiveness and practicality of the peace proposals that have been made and the change in the approach that is needed to resolve the conflict. There seems to be an urgent requirement to address the rights and expectations of the citizens of Israel and the Palestinian territories as well.

Reactions on the ground and internationally

This part requires understanding the reactions of neighbouring and other countries concerning the various peace plans made for the Palestinian-Israeli conflicts. Countries in the vicinity, and more particularly Egypt, Jordan, and Saudi Arabia, along with the other Gulf countries, in the past, have been involved in conflict resolution and peace-making activities and have offered their advice. Some of these changes were made in response to other geographic, political, social, and economic circumstances or the state's interests.

Additionally, the actions and concerns of the UN, the European Union, and the United States have previously been aligned with their approaches to maintaining order in the conflict. These countries have provided funds for and participated diplomatically and, in some cases, directly in the resolution of the holdings in the conflict. These actions have been taken based on the balance of power and other interests, and their concerns for order and peace in the region are not very rational.

The importance of the work carried out by non-market actors like major NGOs and humanitarian and advocacy groups should also be considered in the context of their policy-tailoring work and altering global perceptions. Their fieldwork and participation in global agendas have generated critical debates, exposed human rights abuses, and offered alternative viewpoints in contentious discussions.

The complexities of these regional and global reactions require studying the webs of partnerships, historical ties, and currents of power relations that frame the considerations of the actors concerned. Their positions, interactions, and the particularities of their actions form an important part of the peace plan's context and provide a basis for a nuanced strategy that integrates complex arguments beyond the simplistic dichotomies and blatant assumptions.

Case Studies in Conflict Resolution

In studying the multidimensional aspects of conflict resolution during the Israeli-Palestinian issue, it becomes crucial to examine why certain case studies appear to offer the most relevant insights and directions toward peace. An exemplary case is the Oslo Accords of 1993. These agreements, despite many challenges, provided a basis for mutual recognition, interim self-governance for the Palestinians, and a phased withdrawal of Israeli troops from certain areas of Gaza and the West Bank. Subsequent events, however, showed the violence and disputes that continued to rage around these relics of arrangement and self-governance. Another case study of note is the 2000 Camp David Summit, where the discussions between Israeli and Palestinian leaders brought to the surface some hope, but they were unable to entertain the idea of a true, lasting peace because of the problem of sovereignty over Jerusalem and the borders of a future Palestinian state, as well as the issue of Palestinian refugees. These events from history reflect the complicated and enduring work that must be done to achieve peace in the region, despite such good leadership and support from the world. More positively, it shapes some understanding to examine the negotiable and executed Good Friday Agreement in Northern Ireland as a case.

The power-sharing components of the agreement, the processes of disarmament, and the trust-building measures among the communities have 'lessons learnt' that can be adapted to the Middle East – this is one of the aspects of the agreement that is important. In addition, the change of South Africa from an apartheid to a democratic state illustrates the need for matrices of dialogue, inclusive processes of truth and reconciliation, and transitional justice across deep societal fractures. This case study asserts the need to recognise and address the gaps that result from collective failure to act upon basic justice and the need for a unifying framework to achieve a diverse society. Finally, the post-conflict evolution of Rwanda sheds particular light on the mechanisms of co-existence and reconciliation after the commission of genocide. The building blocks of this framework are the community 'Gacaca' courts, 'national' reparations, and government 'oneness' and 'healing' policies. These individual elements from different case studies highlight how different unresolved issues of conflict are approached and provide a richer understanding of the complexity of conflict resolution. The diverse nature of the conflict studies points to the need for a broad and nuanced understanding of conflict that combines legal, historical, and socio-political thinking. Engaging with these case studies falsifies the notion that peace can come easily and underscores the need to understand the complexity of grievances, require an initiative to engage all stakeholders, and seek ways to address unresolved injustices, promote avenues for dialogue and collaboration, and engage with all parties to promote systemic change.

Pathway to Genuine Peace and Conclusion

In closing, the case studies provide insight into the challenges and varying success of peace initiatives and underline the importance of resolving the core issues and the needs of every side and providing integrative and lasting outcomes. Considering the multitude of conflicts and peace plans and resolutions, it becomes evident that the vision of peace to be constructed for the region under consideration needs to be done with the utmost care, including the historical intricacies, geopolitical sensitivities, and the personal and human side of the conflicts. In contrast to the vision put forth by Mr Trump, the plans for real peace would integrate through the bottom-up approaches the legal, diplomatic, and humanitarian frameworks of the conflicts proposed and merge with the grassroots action at the community level. There is a fusion of humanitarian accountability and bottom-up approaches that defy violence towards integrative justice frameworks. In intersection with these, international law is rigorously respected. Among these, under the core issue, the framework proposed recognises the Palestinian people and, most importantly, the state and self-determination. At the core of real peace, the outlines of justice would, on the other side, involve the deconstruction of inequitable frameworks of the occupation, and the framework, on the other side, democracy of the coexistence that is fair and just. In other words, real peace stipulates a framework of dialogue, trust, and other tangible actions.

Additionally, it requires the active involvement of the global community, addressing the more profound motivations of the conflict, and working for the cessation of discriminatory practices. All relevant parties in the region should emphasise collaboration, economic integration, and cultural exchange as critical aspects of peace that is sustainable. Achieving authentic peace is going to require courageous leadership, devotion to the principles of human rights, and the ability to take on systemic biases and imbalances of power. There is a need for it to transcend the boundaries of temporary self-interests to embrace a unified framework of prosperity and peace for the region as a whole. The road to peace in its truest form is not a question of political calculation or strategy, but more a question of ethics, which the global community should abide by. As we move through this world, trying to find a balance between these areas, we should be reminded of the passion of the people who want a world where people can live together as neighbours. The struggle for peace in its truest form is immensely important for the region and its people, who were once living there in dignity."

2
The Veiled Conflict
Beyond Security and "Terrorism"

Misconceptions and Conflicts – An Analysis and a New Perspective

The history of the concept of the Israeli-Palestinian conflict, and the conflict itself, is likely to overshadow the veritable core of underlying facts that tell a different story. Over a century to date, the conflict has been shaped not only politically but also socially and economically. It is immediately obvious, when placed in context, that both the Israelis and Palestinians have constructed narratives that are intertwined with prejudices and misconceptions that inflame the cycle of violence and enmity. The history of the conflict is constructed with different narratives that have oversimplified the issue and the history surrounding it. To frame the issue politically, there is a need to double argue the set of grievances, the aspirations, and the fears that argue the inner systems of the character attitudinally, both for Palestinians and Israelis. This means that one has to consider phenomena such as the Balfour Declaration, the Arab-Israeli wars, the Oslo Accords, and the extending of Israeli settlements on Palestinian lands. Furthermore, it warrants addressing the psychological outcomes of a chronic conflict, as well as the individual and communal identities, trauma, and memory that come with it.

Histories based on misinterpretations can illuminate how some matters are described and others ignored—a phenomenon that shapes history contrary to the facts to create obstacles to understanding and reconciliation. This chapter attempts to analyse these stubborn misrepresentations of reality and highlight the importance of rethinking the conflict on more plausible and thorough historical grounds. Revisiting history allows one to confront false narratives and develop a nuanced understanding of the Israeli-Palestinian conflict. This is the context of rethinking the reality of the conflict to formulate an approach that is more nuanced and empathetic and goes beyond the historical context.

Security Narratives: Analysing the Political Context

In analysing the narratives concerning security in the context of the Israeli-Palestinian conflict, one is confronted with an intricate web of historical, political, and cultural factors. This section, therefore, intends to break down the major security narratives and try to understand the implications of these narratives in the context of the prevailing politics.

At its most fundamental, the security narrative tends to construct an unbalanced account of the conflict, emphasising the Israeli need for security and disregarding the Palestinian need for security in a more sophisticated and nuanced manner. The critical question that needs to be answered is how these hegemonies have been and continue to be constructed and maintained.

One of the most obvious examples is the Palestinian resistance and dissent, which is framed in the context of the existential threatening violence of the Israeli. The acts of protesting and defending oneself become an attack on the Israeli psyche. It is only by unpacking this narrative that one can understand the structural erasure and disempowerment of the voices of the Palestinian people.

In addition, the combination of security narratives with settler-colonial thinking certainly deserves scrutiny. The creation and growth of Israeli settlements are, in some cases, glossed over and justified by security narratives and policies that dispossess and displace Palestinian peoples. These narratives are important for challenging the deep and structural injustices surrounding the conflict.

Equally important is the global understanding and the support of these security narratives, especially in geopolitical relations and in the framing of news. The global community's collusion in the dominating of these narratives, often at the cost of Palestinian narratives, indicates the far-reaching nature of such discourses beyond the local setting. How these narratives are spread and internalised is essential to understanding the broader relations of power, control, and collusion.

In closing, dismantling the dominant security discourses is crucial for understanding the Israeli-Palestinian conflict in a more nuanced way that goes beyond binaries to address the underlying issues of dominance. The political discourse on security is one that needs engagement in the hopes of moving towards a world that is equitable and just and recognises the common humanity we all share.

Terrorism Labels – Political Tools and Consequences

The use of the term 'terrorism' is not exclusive to the purpose of describing violent acts of particular individuals or groups, and the accompanying context of the use of 'terrorism' is further complicated within the scope of the Israeli-Palestinian conflict. The use of the word 'terrorism' has been a central defensive instrument to attract public attention and then broaden the appeal of the use of a particular frame around a given issue. 'Terrorism' is a label that should be ascribed to given actions or a phenomenon of serious debate, and it requires a thorough understanding that addresses the conflict in its entirety and not in a fragmented manner.

It is important to understand that the assigning of labels, in this case the use of the term 'terrorism', is case-specific and can be a politically motivated label. In the antagonistic situation, one side can consider the actions being taken to be some form of resistance or self-defence, and it is just as easy to position the actions as net acts of terrorism. Such pronouncements fail to provide the concept under consideration with dignity. Furthermore, the context and subjective nature of the phenomena or the actions taken, or of the situation in question, do provide the actor or a given side of the conflict with a set of actions that can be determined to be similar or the same, or of the same nature from which the labels are being questioned.

The significant impacts associated with the use of the term 'terrorism' have a profound effect not just on public perception, but also on international policy and law as a whole. Labelling individuals or groups as terrorists has dire global consequences that can affect their civil liberties and personal freedoms on a basic level, alongside extreme international condemnation.

Within the vast realm of the Israeli-Palestinian conflict, the application of the term 'terrorism' has specifically been associated with the distribution of specific funds, the adoption of particular policies of surveillance and control, and the justification of the use of military force. Therefore, the consequences of such attachments are far more serious than mere rhetoric, as they touch upon the lives of the individuals embroiled in the conflict and the wider international frameworks.

Another aspect is the ways in which the use of the term 'terrorism' serves as a barrier to communication and negotiation. The use of the terms 'militants' and 'fighters' serves the purpose of silencing voices of opposition. This classic and counterproductive use of terminology reinforces perceptions of violence and the use of force in conflicts. It is through the designation of opposition that the most extreme violence is brought to bear, and this hardly represents the voice of peace or a peaceful disentangling of a conflict. These generalisations, more than most, serve as a basis for deepening conflict and hostilities.

Attention and focus on these issues compel one to go beyond the rhetoric surrounding the term 'terrorism' and focus on the core factors leading to such violence. With compassion, we must understand the plight of those caught between opposing views, all tangled together through these incredibly complex polarities. Understanding the even deeper meaning terrorism has in politics and society will help in closing the gap needed to attain peace and further reconciliation.

Daily Realities – Living Under Occupation

The experiences of the Palestinian people remain harsh and complex almost fifty years after the first documented occupation. Occupation involves various issues, including movement and access to everyday necessities, military checkpoints, and various barriers. The right to personal and communal security, stability, and freedom is ignored completely. Under the looming threat of land confiscation, forced displacement, and home demolitions, countless families irremovably grapple with a deep sense of instability and uncertainty. In the daily economic routines, the existence of numerous structural and punitive boundaries to trade, agriculture, and infrastructure severely stagnates the entire economic health of the people, leading to great social and economic distress. Mirror Conflicts, together with the Exposed Settlements, dissect the already existing social inequalities, sustaining utter fragmentation of entire societies. Settled, exposed, and breeding structural violence, the military occupation induces delayed psychological disorders. The people suffer intensely from the permanent state of conflict, immense violence, and strenuous external control over individual liberties.

Children are exposed to conflicts, traumas, and educational disruptions and lose hope for a secure future. Losing childhood among discrimination, hostility, and violence leaves a dent on them and their societies forever. Everyone suffers, but we need to understand and fortify the spirit and determination of the people willing to fight for their freedom and dignity. Even with the difficult day-to-day lives they lead, we need to take their case up with the world to help them remove the burdens all of them face because of occupation.

Media Portrayals – Influence on Global Perception

Global understanding and perception of the Israel-Palestine conflict have a lot to do with how the media covers it. The media pays attention to a story and covers it in a particular way for a specific audience, and the resulting narrative with associated visuals has the potential to drive public sentiment, policy, and international conversations in particular directions. The media's perception and reality distortion ability is substantial because it is the most accessible information for the global audience. But coverage of the conflict and the many viewpoints that come with it needs to be approached with sensitivity, simplicity, and care.

The way a conflict is covered within the media has a lot to do with the 'frame' of the conflict. In framing a conflict, media organisations tend to focus on issues related to security, history, and crises, among others. These issues, especially, shape how "consumers" understand and interpret the conflict, promoting bias and oversimplification. In addition, the use of certain images, words, and stories is responsible for the dissemination of false or misleading information, thus fostering a distorted understanding.

Also, how a conflict is presented by the media has a bearing on both internal and external policies of a state. Public policies concerning media coverage are likely to determine how responsive a government is and how much intervention is put forth, owing to the level of diplomatic and peace efforts needed. Also, the media's exercise of soft power is likely to determine how many resources, humanitarian assistance, and support are provided for the resolution and aftermath of the conflict.

To explore the ways in which the media engages with the Israeli-Palestinian conflict, a focused, accurate, and comprehensive portrayal needs to be given to every facet of the matter while sidelining every omission and marginalised omission in every clouded mainstream narrative of the media. It is also vital to reinforce the need for critical thinking around media portrayals of the conflict. These critical thinking skills are also necessary for the construction and deconstruction of frameworks and arguments in which images of the conflict are manipulated and portrayed so negative biases, misinformation, and propagandistic angles can be extracted.

With the complex scenario which pertains to every global media problem dataset and its ID, the ethics which each local opposition media needs to adopt are multi-faceted; the media mavericks should become locally embedded journalists. Stakeholders should also be equally active in global media morphing to ensure maverick local journalists are cross-broadcasted. This cross-collaboration should result in multi-layered, critical media coverage sculpted in and around all possible angles of the Israeli-Palestinian conflict. Using the now published, maverick dataset, active report bombardment with the cross-collaborated opposition media should become quotidian in every local dataset.

Human Rights Considerations – International Law Perspectives

International law is essential to dealing with the complexities of the human rights issues regarding the ongoing conflict between Israel and Palestine. The Israel and Palestinian conflict is still active and problematic. The web of legal issues regarding this conflict is tricky and convoluted with treaties, conventions, and the principles of international law. Within the legal and ethical international humanitarian discussions, the rights to life, liberty, and security of a person, as well as the right to life, liberty, healthcare, self-determination, and mobility, and the right to education, are neighbouring fundamental rights. In international law, the right of self-determination is essential to the Palestinian people. It remains the focal point of considering the current situation in the region.

The Darfur region of Sudan was the epicentre of violence between 2005 and 2020; the Janjaweed militia frequently attacked largely unarmed civilians, destroying entire villages, and practicing genocidal violence against the non-Arab populations of the region. One of the pivotal instruments in this domain is the 1949 Fourth Geneva Convention relative to the Protection of Civilian Persons in Time of War, which outlines the protections proven to counter the possible abuses civilians might suffer in times of conflict and occupation. Its use against the specific conditions of the occupied Palestinian territories has created much focus and is the subject of legal analysis in international humanitarian law. In addition, the foundational principles and resolutions of the UN, the General Assembly, and the Security Council bear directly on determining the standards of evaluating and addressing the violations of human rights which need to be proven.

The retaliatory mechanisms to hold all the plaintiffs and above defendants accountable to the international legal standards of human rights abuses and violations have led to the framing of defensive mechanisms and courts for the investigations of the breaches. Discussing the place of international criminal law, which targets, indicts, and prosecutes individuals for genocide, war crimes, and crimes against humanity, is part of the overarching discourse of the law and the defence of humanity in relation to long-standing conflicts. Also, the case law spawned from international courts and tribunals, including the International Court of Justice and the International Criminal Court, has richly added to the form of legal jurisprudences of which the internal and external discriminations on human rights during times of war and occupation are case law principles.

Regarding concerns on humanitarian action and the law, the importance of nurturing conditions under which human rights can be violated also holds weight. Everyone, whether directly or indirectly involved in the Israeli-Palestinian conflict, needs to comply with what is required by international law and, in doing so, defend basic human rights and attempt to promote peace in the region. Considering and incorporating the human rights aspects of this protracted conflict as it relates to international law is, indeed, within the necessary actions that can be taken in diplomacy to enhance respect for human rights and equal treatment as a basis for a proper and enduring solution.

Psychological Dimensions – Impact on Palestinian Society

The sociopsychological wounds of the ongoing conflict and occupation have touched virtually every sphere of Palestinian society. The profound and pervasive atmosphere of dread and uncertainty permeating the society has taken a toll on the mental and social health of populations, families, and communities. The almost continuous exposure to deprivation and violence accompanies deep feelings of hopelessness and insecurity. The PTSD, anxiety, and depression disorders of Palestinians have reached alarming proportions. Ongoing trauma exacerbates the delicate sociopsychological balance, transferring the trauma to subsequent generations. The infliction of this kind of trauma produces and manifests in behaviour, relationships, and social structures with a peculiar ease. The way Palestinians relate to themselves and their world beyond them becomes a direct reflection of this profound trauma.

In addition, the dimensions of the conflict inflict damage on the social, educational, and healthcare systems, which directly touch the development of children, psychosocial resilience of the community, and the overall psychological health of the population. The confined feeling in the society is pervasive, as is the feeling of psychological damage that unrestricted access to critical services, opportunities for self-development, and movement infliction cause.

Moreover, the feelings of injustice and inequity brought about by systemic discrimination, marginalisation, and dispossession give rise to indignation because of the profound experiences, thereby strengthening the resolve to resist and self-determine every time.

Even though the mental situation seems to be intimidating, it is important to note that Palestinian society can equally demonstrate resilience and resourcefulness when faced with these obstacles. Individuals and families derive self-worth and empowerment through grassroots projects, community-based initiatives, and culturally tailored mental health support. The invocation of practices and traditions, along with community attachment, helps to counter the deprivation, thereby providing an anchoring mechanism for psychological wellbeing and spiritual sustenance. Additionally, it should be noted that the spirit of the Palestinian people is showcased by the dominating narratives of resistance, resilience, and historic perseverance that counter the prevailing despair. It is important to recognise and integrate these counter-narratives of strength and agency stagnant within Palestinian society to achieve a balanced comprehension of the myriad ways through which the conflict and occupation have been felt. Recognising and acknowledging the profound psychological elements and the society's inherent resilience helps shed light on the society's pathways to healing, restoration, and sustainable peace.

Grassroots Movements – Voices of Resistance and Resilience

The complexity of an ongoing conflict between Israel and Palestine has cloaked various processes of the conflict, spawning the importance of grassroots movements as key players. Local activists and community organisers lead these movements as an essential force to protect and preserve the rights of Palestinians, their violated cultural roots, and the determined ancestral lands.

These movements are a vibrant mosaic of people and groups which advocate for grassroots action, community primary healthcare, practitioners of self-funded, attitudinally based civil non-coercive action, and non policeable activism. Their roles in the conflict are transcendent of traditional and stereotypical expressions of conflict, counter-narrating the stories of Palestinians in occupation.

The primary motivation is to change the state of affairs, attack structuralised and systemised injustice and oppression, and defend the lost and forgotten people sympathetically. Grassroots activists address the demeaning and silencing actions by oppressive structures that systemically and strategically undermine their presence and cause the invisibilisation of the daily hardships of Palestinians.

In addition, grassroots movements strategically navigate beyond conventional geopolitical realms to articulate avenues of impact and collaboration with allies and supporters around the world. These movements utilise social media and digital narratives to unify and share the stories of unwavering courage of the Palestinian people and, at the same time, draw global attention to the Palestinian cause.

The consequences of these movements are not confined to the occupied territories; they also resonate with people and organisations around the world who are concerned with social justice and human rights. This cross-cutting fabric of global solidarity enhances global grassroots movements by fostering cross-cultural understanding and exchange, while simultaneously contesting the dominant narratives of victimhood and disempowerment that the Palestinian community is often subjected to.

Grassroots movements epitomise the Palestinian people's courage and the hope encapsulated within the struggle for justice and liberation. Their tireless attempts to resist oppression across the world are also an attempt to bring forward an era of defiant, resilient struggle that, to these movements, is not bound by geographic limitations.

Efforts in Diplomacy – Negotiating Off the Beaten Track

Efforts in diplomacy regarding the conflict between Israel and Palestine do not go past the Israel- and Palestine-centric arguments and the focus and interest of the other relevant global and domestic stakeholders. This focus also neglects countless other frameworks of negotiation that rest on diplomacy and offer more subtle yet constructive angles of interaction. Most such frameworks are hotbeds of diplomacy that emerge from below the levels of state-civil society, the grassroots, and other outside-the-box approaches, inclusive of state and boundary diplomacy. Appreciating the focus on such non-conventional efforts is crucial to imagine peace and the possibilities thereof in the region.

One such example is the grassroots diplomacy framework that focuses on direct contact and people-to-people engagement at the grassroots level. These initiatives target the interactions of Israelis and people from Palestine and are intended to foster the humanity of the "other" and dismantle the stereotypes, fear and animosity that have characterised and defined the conflict. This type of contact and engagement also brings to the table the notion of trust and the ability to share visions for the future.

Additionally, cultural diplomacy moves beyond artistic and literary endeavours and stretches into the realm of politics. Art, literature, and culture can compose an account of shared humanity and joint ancestry and entwined selves. Participation in artistic activities and cultural exchanges, and international attempts to promote exchanges of exhibitions, film festivals, and artistic collaboration, have tried to create national and stony historical bonds of mutual connection and sympathy, integration, and collaboration, which then bridges the divides between Israelis and Palestinians.

In addition, track-two diplomacy is crucial in this context as well in developing new strategies for dialogue and negotiation. These unofficial, informal channels make room for free and open exchanges of thoughts and ideas and brainstorming sessions well beyond the boundaries of official politics. Retired diplomats, former politicians, or academics typically work in track-II diplomacy, utilising their networks and expertise to give rise to dialogue and ideas which, although uniform and highly structured, are usually absent in the more formalised dealings of state-led negotiation.

In uncloistered affairs of diplomacy levels, women's involvement and contribution in peacemaking and diplomacy are also of great importance and should not be omitted. Women's leadership and active participation in peace processes have shown enormous potential and strength in conflict resolution, sustaining peace building, and producing more inclusive and broad approaches. Recognising the efforts and agency of women in diplomacy is imperative in accentuating the importance of diverse and balanced representation to achieve lasting, just, and fair solutions.

To achieve multidimensional, holistic, and integrative peace building, it is crucial to embrace and weave alternative non-mainstream diplomatic efforts with the rest of the negotiating processes. These alternative processes, designed with the informally authentic civil society and the humane touch, are geared toward augmenting the official formal processes to resolve the Israeli-Palestinian conflict.

Empathy and Understanding: Purposeful Global Divisions

Fostering empathy and understanding within the context of the Israeli-Palestinian conflict means surpassing the binary constructs that limit the scope of discourse at the global level. Bridging the global divides is the product of conscious work toward the demystification of biases and preconceptions, while situating the conflict within its complexities. Mental images of human lives on both sides of the divide are of paramount importance in fostering empathy and understanding in this struggle that is referred to as protracted.

Bridging global divides means embracing this shift and abandoning the divisive discourse that has emerged as the signature of interactions stemming from the conflict. It means deliberately paying attention to consolidating the voices of the vulnerable people who bear the brunt of the impact of the conflict and their narratives. By elevating the human dimension, it opens up the possibility of counteracting the ingrained dehumanising stereotypes, inviting more empathetic responses between and among borders.

Engaging in conflict is an incessant cycle that involves remediating power imbalances framed as bygone grievances, overt discussions spanning the scaffolding injustices, and inequity socially and structurally that have, in one way or another, cut through the conflict. Ignorance and wilful ignorance about the sanctity of the historical and situational context, in addition to power imbalances, is the precise kill shot to understanding the basis for and, subsequently, a nuanced, sincere, accompanied, other-orientated feeling and compassion. It is as much about the colonial violence, dispossession, and dispossession as it is about the encompassing civic security that is rightly, and, in foreign spaces for many, regained by the Israeli population.

The essence of conflict is employing transcendence in feeling and sympathy, that is, through intellectual gazing at bridging global divides. Programmes that aid in fusing cultures, as well as tangential, peripheral, and/or ancillary actions that defy the rationale that exposes individuals to one another, aid the endeavours of the construction above. The phenomena of dialogue, reciprocal pedagogy, and the exchange of life stories as forms of interaction that are relational and not argumentative, eventually, resolve conflict as the interaction moves and lenses to a common humanity that is beyond borders and other elements of geopolitical conflict.

The context of art and literature, along with other more 'seriously defined' forms of social cultural expression, are, in the self-contained and juxtaposed understanding, an unequivocal way to draw upon one's sustaining bones of feeling and understanding towards others. More than just storytelling, in addition to the arts and communal artistic engagements, the bulk of humanity, at the very locus of the inarguable conflict, are connected through the other ends of politics.

To wrap up, any attempt at building an understanding-based bridge to the Israeli-Palestinian conflict will require an understanding of the need to 'humanise' stories told, examine a range of histories, and consider multiple perspectives. Centring the stories of those who have been wronged in historical narratives, facilitating actively supported intercultural contacts, and weaving a mosaic of cross-civilisation exchanges will help cultivate a collective ethos to feel, and at least start, the dialogue based on the touchpoints of unity of our human commonality.

3
Discovery and Promise
The Birth of Gaza Marine

Historical Context – Pre-discovery Gaza

Before the discovery of natural gas deposits in Gaza, the region had a complex socio-political background that had been influenced by historical occurrences and ongoing wars. Gaza was a centre of great significance for commerce and trade and can trace its history back for centuries, being a land of great religious and cultural backgrounds.ABs history was controlled by many of the world's different cultures, such as Babylonians, Egyptians, Greeks, Persians, and the Ottoman Empire, each time putting its own mark on its image and character.

Gaza came to be a British mandate, being a part of the British mandate for Palestine during the period of 1917-1948. Eventually, the escalating tension and contestation between both Arab and Hebrew communities worsened due to a critical situation that led to the outbreak of violence, which resulted in the partition of the land of Palestine. Meanwhile, the formative years of Gaza as we see it today occurred between the years of 1917 and 1967. In fact, during the 1948 Arab-Israeli war, a significant number of Palestinians flocked into Gaza, with some of them forming shifts in its demographics and worsening the region's circumstances while increasing social and economic pressures.

Gaza had been under Egyptian authority for many years until the 1967 Six-Day War, when the territory was occupied by Israel, marking the beginning of an immense Israeli regime. Israeli settlements in Gaza and the occupied territories have led to exacerbated divisions and serious humanitarian concerns. Consequently, this led to the emergence of organised resistance strongholds and the establishment of a Pan-Palestinian identity.

Such troubled historical developments have deep-rooted socio-economic implications for Gaza. The area has suffered from persistent structural and economic underdevelopment, despite its strategic position and vibrant Palestinian histories. Overall, Gaza's situation was characterised by low employment, unstable food supplies, and restricted access to a wide range of necessary sources of nutrition, while a lack of economic and social infrastructure, combined with limited economic opportunities, made living there almost unbearable, leaving Gaza's people feeling truly disheartened and broken when they witnessed their homes and lands being reduced to rubble.

The discovery of natural gas reserves in Gaza occurred at a significant time in the Middle East. This increases the prospects of Gaza being transformed into a potentially flourishing region, providing a more secure condition for the lives of its residents. However, the historical context preceding this revelation underscores the complexities and difficulties that influence Gaza's socio-political landscape, serving as a reminder of the enduring history and the potential for a strong future that the region holds. I regard the natural gas find as a game changer for Gaza, something locals can rely on for their future. These challenging conditions may initially appear to threaten this future but, in fact, represent a tremendous opportunity for progress. Gaza's discovery of natural gas must be viewed as a critical game changer in the lives and aspirations of the people of Gaza. Nonetheless, these difficulties may agitate the mind, as they contain a spark of necessity because there is a jackpot to be won, an opportunity for a breakthrough.

Geological Surveys and First Discoveries

The geological surveys and methods used to search for natural gas in Gaza were crucial for directing the region's energy future. During the initial geological surveys, the subsurface was analysed using advanced tools and technologies to confirm the presence of large deposits beneath the territorial seabed of Gaza. Essentially, these initial findings represented a critical turning point towards achieving energy independence and economic development in the area.

There were geological surveys involving seismic imaging and core sampling that provided geological insight into the area's geological structures and offshore conditions. Geologists and energy experts were therefore capable of identifying prospective reservoirs and making approximate estimates of the gas deposits' bulk. This phase created a foundation for subsequent exploration and production processes, providing guidance on how to utilise the offshore's untapped energy reserves.

It was with great excitement that the confirmation of substantial natural gas reserves off the coast of Gaza was met by the energy industry and the local population hoping for a brighter and more prosperous future. Based on knowledge of the territory's resource potential and these new finds, the discussion about the use of discovery to meet immediate socio-economic challenges and offer opportunities for society has started. Thus, the discovery and examination of these initial gas resources in the field of gas sector planning and decision-making has paved the prospects of squeezing the maximum benefits for of residents of Gaza.

Geological surveys, in addition to other first discoveries, had great political and economic weight. With the additional knowledge that there may be natural gas reserves, international energy companies and governments became interested in the region as potential investment and co-operation partners. This set of developments stimulated discussion about ownership, regulations and etiquette, thereby reminding us that the interaction of this energy resource and regional dynamics is not easy to explain.

As mentioned earlier, the process undertaken for geological investigation and preliminary findings had pulled the distant holes over the broad debate. This has ultimately formed the overall account for the energy geopolitics in the East Mediterranean regarding the management, use and allotment of marine stray gas reservoirs. Hence, the findings of the study see the implication of the study and its relation with the general issue of energy geopolitics in the Eastern Mediterranean, demonstrating the significance of the process of such geological investigation and the preliminary findings.

The Role of International Energy Firms

In the exploration and probable exploitation of the Gaza Marine reserves, the international energy companies have played as significant a part as various other aspects. Their role in the exploration of the area, the first test well results, the approximate financial methods and the political aspects are the crucial ones. Being global energy industry leaders, they have provided both opportunities and woes regarding Gaza's marine boundary prospect as a production field for extracting gas from the ground.

The momentum of the Gaza Marine changed significantly as soon as the world's energy companies joined the project. The use of modern equipment and additional opportunities have created conditions for such an advanced industry, such as expansive geological surveys, initial test drills and seismic trench investigations, which were vital in determining the extent and the quality of the reserves of methane in the area.

The partnership with international energy companies has also provided access to state-of-the-art technologies and expertise in offshore gas development. Through this collaboration, the development of the Programs for Resource Extraction has enabled the operators to ensure operations meet safety and environmental guidelines while achieving maximum efficiency in gas recovery.

Another benefit of partnership with international energy companies is the financial injection into the Gaza Marine project. They have made substantial investments since the genesis of this endeavour, which have served to support the exploration and appraisal activities, including higher expenses incurred in the form of exploration wells, data gathering and feasibility studies. Furthermore, in addition to this, their financial support has boosted investor confidence in the project and has made this initiative more economically attractive to other influential energy industry stakeholders.

Nevertheless, the relationship with international energy companies has brought in more complicated geopolitical issues. Their engagement in the Gaza Marine project explains their connection with Palestine's regional and international political apparatus, which is very delicate. They have various strategic interests and partnerships, which should go hand in hand with broader objectives of diplomacy and not worsen the situation, which is actually tense.

In conclusion, the contribution made by international energy firms to the project known as Gaza Marine has been very significant. The input the firms made in terms of technical capability, the money they spent on the project, and the number of countries in which they operate has greatly affected the project. The issue of international energy firms being included in Gaza Marine has its negatives as well as positives in aspects of global politics. The situation has to be handled well so that its complexities can be mitigated.

Strategic Importance of Gaza Marine

Gaza Marine is situated off the coast of the Gaza Strip. It might be of geopolitical, economic, and developmental help due to the huge amount of natural gas in that area. When exploring natural gas in this area, the biggest entity is the Palestinian Authority, which has Gaza Marine. The PA has the gas field that provides them with the chance to be energy-independent and generates huge amounts of revenue that reduce their dependencies on donors. In this region, the process of exploring for economic alliances and trade agreements might change. Gaza Marine therefore presents the Palestinian Authority with an opportunity to expand their economy as well as bring in foreign investments, create jobs, and increase stability and prosperity in the region. But more importantly, from a strategic point of view, the Gaza

Marine field can significantly influence the negotiations and diplomacy surrounding the Israeli-Palestinian conflict and the region as a whole. As a result, the political landscape of the area that might have been positively affected by efforts towards attaining stability in the Middle East might be altered drastically in a straightforward manner, impacting the area's peace process.

The strategic importance of the Gaza Marine field will shape the response of the international community towards its management. Different actors, including neighbouring countries, international organisations, and global energy companies, have a keen interest in and are observing the fisheries. Besides, Gaza Marine acts as an instrument of regional defence, as it may disrupt existing maritime borders, trigger disputes over sovereignty, or support Eastern Mediterranean partnerships. For a more profound understanding of the complex multinational and regional issues, it is essential to comprehend why Gaza Marine is vital. Thereby, the scrutiny and management of Gaza Marine as a key resource demand careful consideration of the concerned natural lives, aside from all relevant matters of a political nature, economics, and other issues of real significance in promoting stability and prosperity in the zone.

When news broke about Gaza offshore, many hopes rang out in different sectors of politics, social life, and economic life. The announcement of considerable energy deposits off the Gaza coast created significant optimism regarding a game-changing prospect for the area. It signified Palestinians' hopes of avoiding reliance on any assistance, for revenue generated from the gas fields to keep the Palestinian economy afloat and ease energy shortages.

However, amid the high expectations, caution also took

a leading role in the future. Gaza offshore, a part of the Gaza Strip, called for great care, while on the other hand, other areas were seen to have a potential for terrorism. Much of the initial excitement was overshadowed by the ongoing territorial scrambling and security concerns.

Global actors were interested. Many different actors were interested in Gaza Marine on an international scale. Neighbouring countries and international energy companies, among other geopolitical stakeholders, featured in Gaza Marine with their keen interests stemming from their previous successful findings in energy contexts around the world.

Blockade Implications on Development

The Gaza Blockade has deeply affected the development of the Gaza Marine. Without access to the requisite materials, technology, expertise, and even resources offshore, the region's potential to exploit the natural gas reserves is economically unfeasible. Blockade import restrictions severely hinder access to the machinery needed for exploration and extraction. Additionally, the localised instruction and development of personnel needed to operate the gas fields is stunted by limited access to borders in geopolitically complicated regions. Also, the blockade strengthens a paradoxical vision that 'untouched' natural gas rests offshore while the region suffers a blockade-born, unprecedented energy crisis.

The energetic facilities that accompany gas extraction do little to ease the paradox, either. The absence of pipelines, platforms, and processing facilities overburdens gas reserves. Even sluggish processing and logistical borders hinder operational costs. As the local economy prides itself as a self-sufficient, autonomous region, the operational blocks negatively impact development. While the mere sight of this resource is exemplified in the hopes of curbing power shortages and improving the standard of living, the contemptuous blockade conditions of environmental deterioration do encourage the continued deterioration of energy and inflict suffering on the populace that is reliant on the uninterrupted and constant supply of energy. Thus, as a result, this region has been deprived of the economic and social benefits that would have emerged as a direct result of the discovery of the Marine Gaza. The blockade in this case has greatly hindered the possibility of transforming the region's economy and securing energy, as well as expanding employment on a sustainable footing. In addition, the significant delay in utilising these natural resources has region-wide consequences in terms of stability and prosperity, particularly as the region grapples with the ever-present external aid and resources due to the blockade. The case of Gaza is more particular in that it has never been able to break the cycle of dependency and self-sustenance, which unimaginatively is caused due to the blockade. It suffices to say that the blockade's adverse consequences and the remnants of Gaza Marine's development affect the region's economy, infrastructure, energy and, to a greater extent, the dominance of civilisational progress.

Legal and Diplomatic Battles

The legal and diplomatic battles caused by the prospect

of extracting the energy resources found in the Gaza Marine have been ignited ever since. These conflicts centre on clashing assertions of legal rights, along with history and treaties. Sovereign territory, boundary conflicts, and the rule of law involve the deepest of these disputes.

In the midst of geopolitically charged legal situations, the conflicts arise from the offshore resources that belong to Gaza, which is Palestinian – let's not forget it. The unresolved intricacies of the Israel-Palestinian disagreement do little to help, especially according to both parties, who claim ownership of the gas in the sea. The issues of legal dispute that arise, such as "gas in the sea", speak to the more complex issues of territorial sea and EEZ along with the boundaries of the border in the sea.

The search for Gaza Marine puts the boundaries of legal diplomacy to the test. The legal borders of Gaza Marine obligate the user of that space to negotiate with each bordering country, as well as international legal bodies and energy corporations. The legal border of Gaza Marine obligates each user and bordering country to negotiate for that space with each bordering and international legal body, alongside energy corporations. In the complex narrative of joint ownership along with ownership, the politics of resources and the legal relations of bordering countries along with each user grow thicker and more complex.

Additionally, the participation of international actors adds other elements to the diplomatic framework. Legal disputes go beyond the bilateral dimension to global interrelations and global actors. The complexity of diplomatic relations reverberates at several tiers, impacting sub-regional and regional peace and stability, energy security, and the overarching efforts at conflict resolution in the Middle East.

In this vein, the legal and diplomatic disputes over Gaza Marine exemplify the multidimensional relationship of the law, politics, and economics of the region. The settlement of these interrelated issues calls for a blend of legal, diplomatic, and politically calculated actions. While these competing actors construct strategies in the context of the above, the consequences of these disputes will immensely influence the future investment and development of the energy resources of Gaza.

Resource Allocation – Stakeholder Interests

When developing and managing natural resources, the interests of the stakeholders involved can often lead to convoluted discussions. Regarding the Gaza Marine, the potential of tapping into the offshore energy reserves spans across a spectrum of stakeholders and their unique social, political and economic interests, the complexity of which dictates the need to understand and manage the competing interests of stakeholders to achieve fair and sustainable development. Central to the issues being discussed are the competing interests of the neighbouring Israeli authority, the international energy companies, the Gaza local populace and the Palestinian authority all at once. For the Palestinian Authority, tapping into the Gaza Marine energy reserves is a potential means of attaining economic self-reliance and consequently national development. Control of such resources is an invaluable asset in developing a sustainable future state. Contrarily, the strategic interests of Israel in the region fuel controversy regarding the area's maritime boundaries and resources. The situation is further complicated by international energy companies driven by profit, which come at the intersection of the region's political and legal entanglements. Regarding the local populace of Gaza, their interests in the area's resource management and utilisation are equally important.

The worries focus on the socio-economic advantages, the health of the environment, and the possibility of equitable engagement in the decision-making processes. Therefore, the attempts to satisfy these competing interests are multidimensional and complex. It requires open governance, participatory processes, and appropriate systems to guarantee the fair sharing of the profits. Integrated approaches to resolving the competing interests of the stakeholders are key to achieving sustainable development and prosperity in the area. Considering the competing interests creates an opportunity for a rational approach to the development of the Gaza Marine while protecting the interests and welfare of the people concerned.

Technological Challenges and Innovations

While the Gaza Marine gas field is being developed, it is vital to consider the accompanying gas field developments' techniques and innovations. The processes of exploring and extracting resources from the deep sea present several technological challenges.

One of the foremost technological problems is related to the drilling and construction of infrastructures under the sea at considerable distances from the surface of the ocean. The

Gaza Marine development, which is located by the edge of the Mediterranean, requires the use of powerful tools and other appropriate equipment that can withstand high pressure at sea and the other extreme conditions. Engineering subsea systems is another sphere of technological challenge to achieve optimum safety and effectiveness.

In addition, the capture, transport, and storage of extracted materials remain significant technological challenges. Methods of transit over a distance of a few kilometres and the complex seabed geostructure pose major technological challenges. The design and engineering structures for the storage of the resource have to be designed for its specific requirements, alongside the maintenance of safety of the storage.

To evaluate the reserves and the character of the gas reserve of Gaza Marine, the use of advanced seismic surveying and reservoir engineering should be employed. This has to be executed with modern tools and software along with integrated mapping of the geology to provide a constructive engineering outline during the development phases.

In terms of untouched, gas-extraction technologies should be focused on limiting the negative influence gas extraction works have on the marine ecosystem. In the case of fishing and other forms of production, possible advanced ameliorating technologies for the treatment of the waters discharged, and other waste disposal contribute to the ecological safety of the region.

To increase working efficiency and enhance safety during the working processes for the staff and for the resources, considerable progress in the remote observation and command apparatus is essential. The project provides protection, as does the environment, and protective structures are provided for the region adjoining the project due to the quick and efficient capturing and processing of data on possible threatening situations and other emergencies.

Working with important providers of technology and research institutions helps promote innovation in the energy sector. Partnerships and knowledge exchange foster the development of advanced solutions for the challenges posed by the development of Gaza Marine.

Lastly, the development of Gaza Marine demands an unrelenting focus on innovation and excellence in overcoming the complex technological challenges. These challenges can be overcome by pursuing appropriate technological innovations and will in turn assure the success of the project as well as the sustainable development and utilisation of the invaluable natural resources of Gaza Marine.

The Path Ahead – Opportunities and Threats

While tackling aggressive topics geopolitically, the development of Gaza Marine presents both opportunities and threats. In resource development, the depth and shaded particulars of 'opportunity' and 'threat' must be dissected for the more useful nuance that may reside therein. Economically, the resources and the strong energy independence that can be provided can create groundbreaking regional harmony and cooperation. Thus, leveraging the socio-economic development opportunities presented to the Palestinians may alter socio-economic development.

Therefore, ample opportunities can create significant challenges that must be addressed with appropriate caution.

These threats can include, but are not limited to, the geopolitical blockade, competing claims of dominion, and the ever-enclosing complexities of the region. To confront these challenges, the path chosen must be undertaken with the proper resources to mitigate the negative impacts that may occur, through multinational engaging discussions about appropriate and equitable resource allocation. Value must be afforded to set justice, lengthy sustainable development, and knowledgeable respectful harmony among the people. Resources for such frameworks must be justified, and the means of accomplishing them must be justified without contradicting the sustainable development practices to which commitment must be vigorous.

The prospects of Gaza Marine transcend the mere domain of energy; rather, they represent the hopes of the Palestinian people for independence, dignity, and a brighter future.

4
Economics of Denial
The Cost of Blockade

Economic Isolation: Overview

The term 'economic isolation' describes an abstract concept of a blockade functioning as a method of control used by dominant powers over a region or area. To explain Gaza's context, history suggests the blockade began as tension escalated between Israel and Palestine, which ended with the region being gated off and heavily controlling the access and egress of people and merchandise. Geography and historic geopolitical shifts answer the basic questions of 'Why this and why now?' and 'Who benefits?' To Israel, the blockade is rationalised as a way to mitigate the security issues that Gaza militant groups pose, inflating the control over the materials for reconstruction being sent into the region. There is also the Israeli perception that control is a softer method of power that an economy uses to enforce submission, and hostility restraint justifies the policies. Gaza's political elite have also utilised narratives and rhetoric about their perceived defiance against the world and the subjugation of the blockade to bolster their claims, providing justification for the continuation of these policies. Unquestionably, the role of the international community, either in support or opposition in relation to the blockade, is another aspect that complicates the matter geopolitically. The fine line between diplomacy, which is characterised by balancing alliances, and humanitarianism, which has been extended to the encirclement of Gaza, has geopolitically earmarked the region in question. This complex region is characterised by myriad approaches to the problem, including development and promoting human rights, among other innovative measures to resolve the conflict. Thus, one of the key issues regarding the Gaza Strip's economy is the mindset and motives of the policymakers.

Historical Background of the Blockade

The Blockade of Gaza started with the geopolitical environment in the area, fulfilling the criteria of a historical phenomenon. Since 2007, with the capture of Hamas, the split between the Bank of Gaza and the Bank of the West Bank deepened. The Israeli state, along with Egypt and a multitude of other actors, has been fundamental in the enforcement of the blockade—covering the waters, the ground, and the sky. The origins of the blockade are rooted in some primary Arab-Israeli conflicts, with a focus on the looming concerns during the wars in the region. Years following the June 1967 warfare, particularly Israel dominating the remaining territories of Palestine, set the ground for the blockade. These events in history are the foundation blocks for the thick structure of politics, security, and humanitarian issues and help reaffirm the gravity of the blockade for Gaza.

Gaza Blockade Overview and Economic Consequences

The restrictions imposed on Gaza have resulted in and continue to aggravate and create new difficulties for the Palestinian population and its economy. Blockade restrictions have nearly caused the collapse of economic activities, which are now operating at a near-zero threshold. Businesses continue to struggle to operate and almost completely lose out on procurement associated with core activities. Trade deficits and a heavy reliance on imports for essential necessities, combined with import restrictions, have led to the commodification of these goods at exorbitant prices.

Likewise, exclusion from the international market along with imposed trade bans results in decreased economic revenue, inhibiting revenue growth, a paradox to Gaza's economy. The growing underemployment due to invalidation at a sustainable economic growth rate has evoked a sense of poverty among the local workforce. The inability to make ends meet pulls a household below the poverty threshold and has resulted in declining standards of living.

To add, the blockade has slowed progress on necessary construction related to border utilities and services such as healthcare, education, and even sanitation. During this time, public services have suffered greatly, putting the people at significant risk to their health and the environment, creating an ongoing and distressing humanitarian crisis. Consequently, the residents of the Gaza Strip face enormous challenges as they navigate their everyday lives under the strain of economically difficult conditions post-blockade.

Microeconomic effects of this blockade on Gaza include the collapse of livelihoods, small enterprises, and social cohesion. Activism on the border has existed under conditions of economic isolation for an extended period, and those in charge should be aware that their approach is lacking critical aspects that ensure the long-term well-being and development of the people of Palestine.

Disruption of Trade and Commerce

The blockade on Gaza has severely disrupted trade and commerce, resulting in an unstable and unprosperous economy for the region. Due to the blockade, imports and exports to and from Gaza have been significantly reduced, making trade with the outside world challenging. Essential goods for the people of Gaza have become unaffordable and even inaccessible, which stagnates the region's economy. Not only does the region's economy suffers, but the people also face unemployment, as the inability to market goods means the region cannot generate any revenue.

The effects of the blockade extend beyond the market and trade within the region. It has distorted the region's trade networks and disrupted associated businesses. Businesses in Gaza have to confront a scarcity of raw materials and machinery, which has reduced the region's production. The economy continues to suffer, and the people remain jobless. The inability to market goods means the region cannot generate any revenue. Suppliers of goods are required to pay local businesses, which further compounds the economic challenges in the region.

The blockade has economically isolated Gaza, denying it the potential benefits of international trade and innovations from the global marketplace. The absence of trade stifles any private sector attempts at diversification, meaning the lack of trade perpetuates technological dependency and resource impoverishment.

With the private sector losing its competitive edge, it becomes the primary employer, while the blockade has imposed deflationary pressures on the economy. A loss of sales translates to a loss of job openings, and economically frustrated Gaza finds itself caught between sky-high unemployment and even sparser underemployment, while a lack of funding stifles individual attempts at self-employment. Any semblance of a functional economy serves as a deterrent to investment.

The trade-blocked polity burdens the self-employed with income and wealth disparity. Lost trade opportunities diminish earning potential, while the polity's trade restrictions affect the availability of necessities. The overall sense of economic hopelessness has managed to close down Gaza as a society, while beyond an average temperament, only a few can dream of its well-being.

To summarise, the blockade has significant economic consequences, such as the disruption of trade and commerce in Gaza, with its impacts leading to restricted trade and the global inability to conduct business, which in turn results in a loss of business productivity, an increase in job scarcity, and a worsening of economic inequality in the region. All these issues require a detailed plan that actively bridges the gap between sustained economic growth and trade, as well as implementing other policies for shared prosperity.

Impact on Employment and Livelihoods

This blockade has wide social and economic consequences for the people working in Gaza. Activities that the blockade limits, such as the movement of people and goods, as well as capital, have resulted in many losing the possibility of having a job and the means by which employment can become available. Without external means from other countries, capital, and resources, local businesses are forced to a standstill, which results in reduced wages and a high number of layoffs. Many people are forced to accept informal employment, which leads to the collapse of family structures and social environments.

In addition, as a result of the blockade, there has been a reduced expansion of key economic productive sectors, such as agriculture, due to the impeded development of economic productive and social infrastructure, including both services and construction activities. The decline in employment opportunities also impacts the prospects for economic diversification and recovery and for sustained development, as well as diversification stagnation. All these economic features in Gaza result from the cycle of economic stagnation, which increases the underlying vulnerability of households and heightens humanitarian aid dependency. With these factors at play, aid dependency becomes a never-ending cycle.

The economically active demographic of the population has suffered the most, facing a lack of real upward mobility and employment opportunities. Due to a lack of meaningful work, the gap of disenchantment widens, alongside productivity, potential for aggressive action, and propensity for social disorder becoming much higher. Therefore, the impact of economic employment opportunities is felt socially and politically much more than in the case of the blockade's reasoning behind it.

The employment crisis, which the blockade exacerbates, is missing the critical dimension of pervasive gender inequality, where the disparity between women and men is most pronounced. With the closure of markets and increased mobility restrictions, discriminatory practices and lost market opportunities have intensified, meaning that women, even with low economic engagement and being vital components of the household, have encountered greater barriers. Within Gaza, the limited range of employment opportunities disproportionately presents a female challenge, as it dramatically curtails their autonomy, deepens employment gender inequality, and widens the inequity of socio-economic gender relations.

The negative impacts of the blockade on employment and livelihoods present a multifaceted challenge that encompasses social, economic, and even humanitarian concerns. Purposeful and focused actions are necessary to address the critical issue of the employment gap. These include targeted investments with employment goals, inclusive economics, and the active removal of barriers and restrictions across various domains. Overall, the employment gap is the most urgent area for action. This issue poses an even greater challenge if the blockaded territory is to be considered. Greater concern is warranted for this blockaded territory, as it allows for minimal incomes through gradual, eased, and sustainable economic pathways, alongside active attempts to reduce both concealed and overt socio-economic shackles.

Humanitarian Consequences and Aid Dependence

The blockade has caused significant humanitarian suffering and strikes at the essence of daily life in the Gaza Strip. Healthcare is a critical sector that has suffered due to the blockades on vital life-saving medicines and the controls on the imports of other necessary goods. This is the reason the blockade has been a cause for concern even to humanitarian organisations trying to provide the much-needed 'boots on the ground' aid and assistance. This has made the population reliant on foreign handouts as international aid. This international aid is given at the cost of political leverage, silencing an entire community. Communities built on political control and egress tend to lose their self-sustaining strength. This loss compromises the community's self-reliance. This form of aid dependency is also economically tragic. The community is keener to borrow and spend foreign capital without creating self-sustaining, economically viable structures first. The economic tactics adopted become deleterious political internecine.

The dependence has also exposed the community to geopolitical indignities and has caused an immeasurable deficit of basic decency. Educational opportunities and materials fostering social intelligence have also been blocked. The subsequently unchecked growth in frustration only becomes a factor which eases the further political domination. Helplessness and loss of economic dignity become a collateral cause of political control. This has not only eclipsed the well-being of the spies in an entire community, losing their dignity in the process. The most suffering aspect is the psychological cycle of further damaging their self-worth through basic indignities such as loss of hope.

The ongoing catastrophe in Gaza brings different issues with its humanitarian aspect, and the consequences of the blockade should be considered, and the whole aspect of aid should be treated with the utmost importance in terms of sustainable strategies and advanced development. New approaches should be taken in which aiding local activities, regaining self-determination, and balancing their integrated approaches which operationalise these tenets in a way that enhances human rights, security and dignity.

Impact on Construction and Development

The blockade Gaza is under enables dire humanitarian and economic mismatches and also creates stress on the whole area in terms of construction and above development. Development in construction that includes the necessities like water and proper sanitation, healthcare and even teaching facilities has because of the blockade, little prospect for development in construction.

The blockade has immensely allowed the area to develop economically but stifled the area with hovering bridges and crippling roads that support basic activities. What is more, the blockage endangers people by vanishing basic water and proper sanitation, which amplifies the suffering people go through.

Also, the blockade severely limits Gaza's ability to develop further. The failure to import necessary raw materials, as well as the technology and equipment, stifles innovation and the evolution of new industries. Development is constrained by the lack of equipment and resources, preventing the formation of human capital and intellectual development. Thus, the absence of development projects diminishes the chances of economic diversification and growth in Gaza.

The unending fragmentation of infrastructure and development remains an underdeveloped and exposed set of Gaza's growth within a global context, supporting the notion that the region can't stimulate self-sustained growth. The development of infrastructure and facilities to support economic growth is Gaza's unfulfilled promise. For future generations, these are basic migration pathways that will spark innovation and growth that are part of the forward set of arms.

The blockade's impact on the social and economic stagnation of Gaza is set in international policies, and within the region, the stunting of development sets the region in a lower stasis, reliant on aid and needing the construction of base infrastructure that will set Gaza within. Support and coordination from the international community are needed to assist in the construction of vital infrastructure that is the base set of arms for continued growth within the region.

The Impact of World Sanctions

The world's economic sanctions on Gaza have impacted Gaza's economic condition while worsening the already existing situation due to the blockade. These sanctions are traditionally imposed against certain governments or officials, but their effects trickle down to the ordinary people and society at large, resulting in net negative welfare consequences. Gazans have already been suffering due to the absence of essential economic order resources and the available economic opportunities, and the negative economic impact of the Gaza blockade further exacerbates the situation. The above concerns, coupled with the sanctions due to political issues, are counterproductive to the Gazans and undermine the very purpose of keeping humanity above and beyond politics. Hence, humanity and its welfare must reflect on the purposes of such measures, and it must be examined whether the measures purported to achieve such purposes are in the people's interests. Analysing the international sanctions imposed on Gaza, it becomes evident that instead of fulfilling the political purpose, these international sanctions deepen poverty conditions, restrict available essential welfare services, and limit funding available for sustainable development services. The international community's lack of capacity while imposing the international sanctions often blocks humanitarian assistance, further increasing the entrenched order of economic dependence.

As this section explores the depths of international sanctions, one must focus their analysis on the consequences of the sanctions on the sectors of health care, education, and commerce. The combination of the blockade and the sanctions and their impact on the socio-economics of Gaza should be a concern for the international defenders of human rights and global policymakers. This study seeks to provoke further analysis regarding the moral issues surrounding the deployment of economic sanctions and their impact on bilateral relations. The nuanced relations of international sanctions and the Gaza population reflect the need for a sophisticated explanation of the sanctions, which should embody humanitarian values over political dominion. It is important to highlight that balanced scrutiny and analysis of the international sanctions can aid in the development of rational policies regarding the international sanctions so that rational decisions in policies respecting social justice and the well-being of the people who suffer from international political relations become the main policies in use.

Case Studies: Industries Affected

When considering the economic impact of the blockade on Gaza, it is necessary to examine particular case studies that highlight the disproportionate impact on different industries and sectors of that region. The case studies demonstrate the complexity of the blockade and the obstacles it creates for Gazan businesses attempting to operate sustainably. One case study focuses on the agriculture industry, which was once the backbone of Gaza's economy. Local farmers have suffered significant losses, leading to food insecurity and the collapse of livelihoods for many families. This is a direct result of import and export sanctions on essential resources such as fertilisers and irrigation equipment, along with export restrictions. Additionally, severe restrictions placed on construction and manufacturing industries have resulted in greater infrastructural developmental lags, coupled with rising unemployment among a sizeable educated segment. The region's productive capacity has taken a serious hit. This stagnated economic growth and kept the region reliant on humanitarian aid. The shifting restrictions on the Gazan fishing industry, coupled with naval limits, have devastated the region's economy. Fishermen are now unable to feed their families.

Particular case studies illustrate the extensive effects the blockade has on traditional ways of life and economic activities. They also point to the lack of sufficient transformative attempts and the importance of sustainable methods to engage the economies of the disrupted industries and to once again make the region economically sustainable. The merging of personal stories and empirical evidence of the affected people provides a wider perspective on how these matters need to be approached and handled from both national and international viewpoints. These stakeholders also need to understand the additional value that is lost by continuing to economically isolate and blockade Gaza.

Conclusion: Long-term Implications and Global Perspectives

The economic blockade has implications that are long-range and extend to matters outside the region and into the rest of the world. The economic effects on Gaza are compounded by the purposeful limiting of access to exports and imports and access to basic goods and services, which puts the entire region on the brink of an impoverished state. The economic and humanitarian challenges of the region are exacerbated by the blockade, whose resources are steadily being denied. The protracted crisis has many layers, each of which the international community is aware of and is steadily grappling with. However, time and again, the Gaza blockade seems to impact the world on many levels.

Disregarding the issues at hand, the economic isolation of the Gaza Strip from the rest of the world raises profound questions about the nature of humanitarian support, international law, the role of the world in dealing with such issues, and Gaza's relationship with the international community. The blockade to which Gaza is subject is a major barrier to peace and stability in the Middle East region. It is, however, fundamentally more than that. It is a mark of great inequity and a gulf of social and economic imbalance in the world.

It speaks to the injustice and unequal treatment which is meted out to those people who are in dire need of support. The world over, people are in desperate need of justice and equality. The suffering and impoverishment that the blockade inflicts on the people in the region of Gaza, extending beyond its borders, are worrisome.

Regardless of how the world overlooks these challenges, the blockade and its economic ramifications worldwide are complex and disturbing from a humanitarian perspective as well. The issues of Gaza are not mere problems which the Gaza region and its inhabitants need to grapple with and resolve. The persistent social and economic marginalisation, denial of human dignity, justice, democracy, and the blockage of a whole society's potential are issues which will inevitably need to be addressed by the international community. The social and political ramifications and the psychological wounds which will need to be healed are, to be blunt, a legacy that is unworthy of passing down to younger generations. The legacy of the younger generation is what they will need to shape the overall paradigm of peace and stability for the world in the coming years.

The global policy and diplomacy systems require immediate rethinking. The economic and moral costs of the blockade demand that the UAE give precedence to human welfare and human rights in all dealings. It requires an understanding of sustainable economic deprivation and outlines a strong description of the suffering and deprivation that the populations in conflict endure, emphasising a strong and urgent commitment to multilateral cooperation and intervention.

Disregarding the long-term effects of the blockade on Gaza necessitates reflection on the underlying issues of justice, human fellowship, and global interconnectedness. This chapter is intended to mobilise the rest of the world on the issue of Gaza and to encourage the world to accept its responsibility in tackling the issue and working towards the dignity and fundamental rights of all people, in a geopolitically neutral manner.

5
Maritime Rights Under Siege
UNCLOS and Palestinian Claims

Overview of Maritime Law and Its Relation to UNCLOS

The provision of maritime law is a specialisation of public international law, and it concerns itself with the international relations of states in all areas of the world and in the ocean. Central to maritime law is the United Nations Convention on the Law of the Sea (UNCLOS). It covers an entire legal span of all the oceans, from the territorial sea to the deep seabed. It is the Convention that embodies the principal goals of maritime law. Thus, it strives to provide legal certainty, facilitate peaceful relations, and conserve the marine environment.

One feature of UNCLOS is the delimitation of maritime boundaries, which include territorial waters and exclusive economic zones (EEZs). Within the territorial waters, the coastal state has complete sovereignty, control, and jurisdiction over a reasonable area, which extends to 12 nautical miles from the shore. Beyond the territorial waters are the EEZs, which extend to 200 nautical miles, where the coastal state has exclusive rights to exploit and manage the resources. In general, UNCLOS provisions aim to establish national jurisdiction boundaries in marine space and foster peaceful maritime relations.

Moreover, UNCLOS establishes limits for the peaceful settlement of disputes related to the interpretation and implementation of maritime law. This is vital in ensuring maritime stability and lawfulness.

The potential for heightened tensions is alleviated, and the disputes can be resolved peacefully due to the incorporation of a systematic framework intended to constructively handle competing claims of a maritime nature. The importance of UNCLOS is also acknowledged because a substantial majority of the international community has ratified and is abiding by its principles and obligations. The existence of this consensus substantiates the fact that there is indeed a need for a comprehensive framework to be able to manage law and order over the oceans.

The provisions of the convention can be said to form the pivot of UNCLOS when its importance is being dissected. The provisions of UNCLOS not only set the boundaries of the national jurisdiction but also enable the cooperative engagement of the countries in the region, which contributes to the enhanced sustainable development and management of the region's marine resources. At the same time, UNCLOS is a basic instrument for the fostering of stability, security, and peace in the region, providing the basis for the cooperative and equitable control and use of the maritime space. The more we examine the historical context of the maritime claims of Palestine, the more we feel the need to celebrate UNCLOS and its richness, especially in relation to the dominating currents of maritime law and geopolitics.

Contextual Background for Palestinian Claims Graphical Area

The Israeli-Palestinian conflict, as well as the wider geopolitics surrounding it, provide the context for Palestinian maritime claims. Most have not focused on the claims as particularly salient, historiographically, because the claims revolve around the primary face of the conflict, which is territorial. The Palestinian territorial waters have historically faced varying degrees of restrictions and Israeli control, which have obstructed the Palestinian coastal communities from gaining full control. The Palestinian coastal communities' loss of access to the sea as a result of the 1948 Israeli state formation has had a series of ripple effects on their maritime access and rights for the population hinterland to the coastal territories. The Israeli state formation, with its attendant regional realignments, disputes over borders, and of course, over military rule, has systematically erased Palestinian claims to the sea. The absence of, and the loose anchor onto, Palestinian maritime sovereignty has strung together Palestinian coastal communities and fishermen into a web of institutionalised underdevelopment and deprivation.

The past of Palestine in relation to the sea should be considered to construct a balanced solution that resolves the legacy of dispossession while aiming to strengthen the Palestinian agency over self-governance and over the sea resources and management. Maritime governance injustices should be attainable to provide a sustainable base for possible future frameworks which aim to develop the Palestinian coastal areas for use. Furthermore, the emphasis on the historical context of the claims will aid the Palestinians in dealing with international legal treaties and instruments that seek to address the age-old inequities of unfair access to and use of maritime resources. This underscores the need for a more holistic approach to the Palestinian claims concerning the sea to achieve a more balanced solution, which also underscores international legalities and the maritime entitlement of the Palestinian people.

Legal Framework: Principles Emerging from UNCLOS Regarding Palestine

The United Nations Convention on the Law of the Sea (UNCLOS) is the first of its kind to establish an international legal framework for the delimitation of boundaries and the accompanying maritime rights of any given country. It remains central to the philosophy and policies relating to the use of the oceans and seas and to the regulation of economic activities and the environment. For Palestinians, especially those exercising rights to maritime claims and resources, the principles outlined in UNCLOS are of enormous importance. For Palestinians, the legal principles contained in UNCLOS are critically important because it deals with the delimitation of boundaries, the regulation of maritime activities, and in particular, the protection of the marine environment.

The principles of UNCLOS which are most important to the Palestinians are the concept of Exclusive Economic Zones (EEZs), in which the coastal states are granted sovereign rights to explore, exploit, conserve, and manage the resources of more than two hundred (200) nautical miles from their coast. This is particularly important to the Palestinian people as it concerns their ability to utilise and control the marine resources of the Eastern Mediterranean. Moreover, UNCLOS has provisions for the determination of the continental shelf, which impacts the delineation of resources lying on the seabed beyond the EEZ.

In addition to this, UNCLOS fosters interstate collaboration to resolve disputes concerning borders and their subdivision through legal frameworks and endorses the peaceful resolution of such disputes. This consideration is especially relevant to the case of the Palestinian people because of the intricate regional dynamics and the competing claims in the Eastern Mediterranean. Knowledge of the mechanisms of dispute resolution provided under UNCLOS is beneficial to the Palestinians, as it enables them to pursue international legal recourse and resolve their disputes peacefully.

Apart from this, the convention stipulates the protection and enhancement of the marine environment and defines the management of marine resources together with their environment that requires protection and sustainable development. This also serves the interests of the Palestinians in fostering the balance of the ecosystem and the responsible stewardship of the marine space under their authority. Using the environmental provisions of UNCLOS, Palestinians can highlight the importance of ecosystem preservation and sustainable development in their maritime activities.

In closing, understanding and using UNCLOS is crucial for Palestinians to exercise and effectively manage their coastal waters. This international treaty guarantees access to ocean resources and establishes a framework for resolving conflicts and fostering collaboration between countries. Palestinians, with the support of UNCLOS, would be able to intelligently manage the challenges of international and maritime law and use the principles of international law to defend their claims while ensuring good governance over their maritime territory.

Regional Conflicts and Their Consequences in Palestinian Waters

Almost every maritime boundary along the Eastern Mediterranean coast is part of complicated regional disputes, including the adjacent Palestinian waters. When offshore gas reserves were discovered, tensions intensified, and gas became an object of competing claims and interests. Henceforth, the zeal of claimants, which includes Israel, Lebanon, Cyprus, and Turkey, is now extended to offshore maritime claims which satisfy certain presumptions of hydrocarbon wealth. Their overlapping claims and maritime disputes are bound to have serious consequences on Palestinian waters due to the exclusive economic zones and overlapping claims on the potentially resource-rich regions. These disputes have no solution because of the untangled paradoxes of the region and the deeply rooted political tensions. The gap of clarifying and redefining cross-border conflicts, coupled with the continuous violence and the absence of peace treaties, makes it all the more unsolvable. The Palestinian sovereign authority is responsible for managing and controlling hydro-resources, but existing conflicts limit their ability to defend their interests. These conflicts have, on the other hand, diminished the economic and social potential which lies in their waters through suppression and acute control. The intensifying regional armed conflict and surveillance over the Eastern Mediterranean serve no other purpose. The absence of consensus and certain reasonable negotiations on the respective lines of boundary, resource allocation, and ownership serve to exacerbate instability and volatility in the Palestinian maritime spectrum. It is crucial to understand the relationship between these regional conflicts and the Palestinian waters. We should address these geopolitical complexities to establish a legal framework that empowers the Palestinians to safeguard and enhance their waters.

Challenges Faced by Palestinian Authorities in Exercising Maritime Rights

Exercising Palestine's maritime rights comes with its own set of challenges, which stem from the geopolitics and law concerns of the Israeli-Palestinian conflict. Palestinian authorities are overwhelmed with issues, having little to no control over the waters, which means the ability to manage and use the waters is nonexistent. Strained access to these waters by Israeli naval vessels, coupled with Israeli restrictions, adds to an already difficult Palestinian economy, which is steadily being starved of growth. There is no functioning, centralised Palestinian government, which further removes any decision-making structures, which adds to the burden of having to fight these maritime conflicts. The absence of control and responsibility is accompanied by complete fragmentation of policy structures. This further underscores Palestine's lack of growth in the sea economy. There is minimal control over these waters, having little defensive and offensive naval assets; the lack of investment is almost shocking. Loss of investment in construction of power and infrastructural assets in these seawaters adds to the inability to trade with other countries, further reinforcing the lack of economic growth.

In addition, the lack of stability and the ongoing security issues in the region severely limit maritime activities, risking potential investment and strong regulatory frameworks. The core problem is the attempt to claim and protect Palestinian maritime rights in the face of multiple geopolitical, legal, and economic complications. Apart from this, it is essential to recognise the need for cooperation and partnership among the constituents to attend to these issues for the progress of offshore Palestinian resources. Formulated policy, combined with investment in institutional increases and the Palestinian authorities' advancement of international relations, will help serve their interests by overcoming these challenges. This, in turn, will benefit the entire region and not just the Palestinian people.

Case Studies: International Precedents and Their Relevance

When looking into the maritime claims of the Palestinians, the South China Sea maritime boundary dispute should also be looked into. This dispute is distinct because of the numerous countries involved and the global attention it has attracted. The South China Sea Arbitration, which deals with the Philippines vs. China, and the subsequent actions of China, illuminates the use of international law in the contested waters of the South China Sea. Likewise, the case of the United Kingdom and the Chagos Archipelago, which deals with the question of British sovereignty over the islands and the claims of the Republic of Mauritius, is emblematic of the myriad complications that arise in the process of decolonisation and the assertion of the emancipated nation's right over contested waters. The circumstances surrounding these cases reveal parts of the complex relationship between international law, relevant international legal institutions, and the profoundly impactful geopolitics that cascade over the people involved. Within such an overarching geopolitical and maritime international system, the Palestinians' right to the adjacent waters of their territory is hardly an exceptional or isolated claim. Having understood the international law pertaining to these other cases provides a specific context in which the other case law is useful to predict redress for the particular grievances of the people.

Exploring these studies allows us to recognise similarities, extract key strategies, and shed light on the intricate issues of maritime jurisdiction and sovereignty. They also illustrate how to use advocacy, diplomacy, international organisations, and alliances to assert and protect maritime rights. The analysis of international case studies and their relevance reinforces the need to consider Palestinian maritime claims alongside the rest of the principles and instruments of international law and diplomacy. This analysis enables evaluation of the extent of judicial recourse, prospects of negotiated settlements, and the custodianship of Palestinian maritime rights.

Geopolitical Tensions: Israeli Restrictions on Palestinian Access

Geopolitical tensions between the Israeli and Palestinian territories have substantially restricted Palestinian access to maritime resources. The Israeli barriers on Palestinian access have posed, and continue to pose, many obstacles for the Palestinian authorities and the population that relies on the sea for their livelihood. As for the Palestinians, their most pressing concerns have to do with the imposition of unilateral Economic Exclusive Zones (EEZ) by Israel and its control over strategic sea regions. This control, coupled with the lack of access to the so-called coastal waters, has adverse effects on fishing, marine commerce, and the growth of offshore energy resources. The application of naval blockades and arbitrary restrictions on Palestinian fisheries has been intensified, leading to direct confrontations at sea where people get hurt while pursuing their occupation at sea and to their peril and the safety of people engaged within the waters. Mediterranean, the Israeli Navy has not only restrained the further funding of the economy but has also the growing distrust and tension of the neglected, and the rest of the region ached, and the region of meridian tension ached.

Additionally, the absence of precise legal definitions of the sea borders and competing assertions of sovereignty between Israel and Palestine have sparked disputes and conflicting legal frameworks that impede Palestine's ability to freely navigate and control and actively dominate her maritime domain. Such legal and administrative complexities have made the maritime domain problematic and the remnants of dystopian control of Israel difficult to sustain and develop. Inheritance of dystopia: the remnants have hardly controlled Israel, and there is imbalanced maritime domain control of Palestine that borders the Palestinian region.

The marginalising and eliminating disparity of sea-bottom and sea waters freely and disproportionately accessible has unfavourably transformed the socio-economic order within Palestinian and Israeli entities on a larger scale and in more complex ways of inequity. Manipulating over controllable maritime borders of Palestine along with patentable borders that are not controlled over has enabled the region. Resolving Israel's restrictions on the Palestinian people alongside the geopolitical tensions that come along with it is not an easy task. This issue needs to be resolved by having positive communication, international legal frameworks, and sharing the resources fairly. Israel and the Palestinians need to understand that there are interrelated maritime resources that, if properly managed and shared, can alleviate the tensions and create an environment that is conducive for both to prosper.

Implications for Palestinian Economic Development

The implications concerning the siege, maritime rights and Israeli restrictions on Palestinian access have serious consequences for Palestinian economic advancement. Considering the Gaza Strip is densely populated, coupled with other pressing socio-economic challenges, the maritime sector's resources could be a game changer for economic and sustained development. Israeli restrictions, the naval blockade, and limitations on fishing zones, however, undermine these opportunities.

The maritime sector provides the Palestinian population with significant employment opportunities. Fish stocks, other marine resources, and hydrocarbons could spur development in fishing, aquaculture, and offshore energy industries. These industries would be capable of fulfilling not only the domestic market but also the needs of the surplus-producing market, thereby assisting in the advancement of the

Palestinian economy.

Constructing maritime trade capabilities and port infrastructure will improve Palestine's connectivity and international trade. Investment in Palestine's strategically located coastal region enables trade with neighbouring countries and beyond, thereby enabling economic diversification and integration. Eventually, such investments will induce the growth of Palestine's maritime economy, making the country a competitive region in the import-export market, thus enhancing economic diversification.

In addition, Palestine's untapped maritime resources have the potential to drive investment and innovation. The investment and innovation will probably drive growth in the fields of marine research, science and technology, as well as in marine sustainable resource management and marine environment protection. Not only will those gains strengthen and improve the competitive edge of the Palestinian economy, but they will aid in global sustainable development and protection efforts as well.

Even so, the untapped economic development potential placed on Palestine because of the restrictions placed upon it hinders the upside potential for investment. Palestine's lack of access to the open seas and lack of shipping access stifles investment in the country, thus stagnating the economy. Such a condition strengthens the economic dependency and stagnation, leaving the nation as unprosperous and lacking in self-sufficient growth.

To improve the Palestinian economy, the effects of the limits on Palestinian maritime rights must be addressed. The mere recognition and respect of these rights, and the resolving of geo-strategic access barriers, will permit the unleashing of the maritime domain's propulsive capacity for sustainable economic development in the region. This will, in the long run, help achieve the much-cherished goals of the Palestinian people, which include self-determination, economic development, and peace.

International Advocacy and Support for Palestinian Maritime Claims

The quest for international support for the Palestinians' maritime claims has, in turn, advocated for their recognition and protection, serving to disappoint the Palestinians' international legal rights. Advocacy support has been a primary strategy ever since. Diplomatic avenues have been pursued for Palestinian advocacy in international relations with the legal support of the Palestinian cause, framing it under the United Nations Convention on the Law of the Sea (UNCLOS). Henceforth, the roles of NGOs, advocacy, and international legal scholars in the "maritime rights of Palestinians" advocacy have been emphasised in defending and amplifying the voices of the oppressed. In this context, significant support for Palestinians' claims has come from public opinion, advocacy within international legal sub-systems, and strategic lobbying by intergovernmental organisations that undermine counterclaim responses. Furthermore, advocacy for Palestinian claims under international law, supported by the United Nations, the International Court of Justice, and regional blocs, has been pivotal in shaping their regional peace efforts while attracting worldwide attention. Advocates have emphasised the importance of support, framing Palestinian activism with the goal of achieving international unity in responsive advocacy.

Furthermore, support from powerful countries and forming partnerships with allies has strengthened the legal basis for the Palestinian claim to territorial waters, as well as the moral and legal case for the injustice suffered by the Palestinian people. The unification of legal practitioners concerning the advocacy of people and the bottom-up movement has generated, as it were, a mushrooming of support that goes beyond national and political borders. Proponents of the movement use both overt and covert campaigning based on its main tenets to shift the focus of international advocacy towards Palestinian territorial waters, aiming for a balanced recognition and restoration of rights. Still, the focus of the advocacy and the international support of the advocacy should continue to be aimed at reframing the paradigm and empowering the Palestinian people to address the intricacies of the maritime dispute, negotiating with tenacity and endurance.

Conclusion: Navigating Toward a Resolution

To put it another way, the difficulties concerning the Palestinian Chamber, associated with the legal, geopolitical, and economic spectrums, are impactful and call for an active centre of attention. International advocacy is necessary for the recognition and protection of Palestinian claims on the sea. International support, while critically important, should be complemented, for the effective assertion and protection of maritime rights, with a domestic consolidation of the Palestinian rank and file. What is additionally, and perhaps above all, of central importance is the cultivation of a legal rationale because of the United Nations Convention on the Law of the Sea (UNCLOS) as a key instrument to advance claims accompanied by the Palestinian territorial sea and adjacent maritime zones and the resources therein. Palestinian negotiators should be prepared to couple any attempts at dispute settlements with offers of cooperative arrangements for the management of overlapping and adjacent resources to the maritime zones. Crucial, perhaps, is the humanitarian case, which will strategically add to the arguments for unrestricted maritime access, development, and endeavours for the people of Palestine. From this perspective, it will be easier to gather support for the cause. In addition, there is a need to advance the technical and infrastructural capability for the careful and intermingled development of marine resources to foster further development prospects for the people of Palestine.

The global community has gained awareness of how disparate political and geostrategic issues are interconnected. This makes the moment right for advocating for Palestinian maritime rights. Eventually, the perspective of Palestinian political entities as well as the rest of the globe will be essential in constructing the line of dominance in resolving the issue with a balanced approach to justice, equity, and the rule of global law. If the Palestinian political elite addresses the issue with measurable effort and deploy the right tools and alliances, there is an attainable pathway to achieve the full set of maritime rights.

6
Israel's Toolbox of Obstruction
From Blockade to Exploitation

Historical Overview of the Blockade

The imposition of blockades has been a recurring strategy in international relations starting from ancient times. As a means of imposing economic and political pressure or achieving military goals, blockades have been used throughout history. In modern times, blockades, particularly within the Israeli-Palestinian conflict, are the result of a web of history, territorial disputes, and issues of geopolitics. Blockades within Gaza have a history starting from the Six-Day War in 1967, when Israel gained control of the Gaza Strip and the West Bank, East Jerusalem, and the Golan Heights. The 'Oslo Accords' of the 1990s, which created the Palestinian Authority and a proposed resolution for the Israeli-Palestinian conflict, left the status of the Gaza Strip unresolved. In 2007, during the violence and political instability of the Israeli-Palestinian conflict, Israel implemented a naval blockade to restrict arms entering Gaza. This blockade was intensified later on when Hamas won the election and created a split control over the Gaza Strip and West Bank with Fatah.

This unfolding in history underlines the interwoven multiplicities of security problems, domestic Palestinian politics, and the overarching strategic Israeli calculations. The legal and humanitarian issues of the blockade, its imposition, and persistent extensions fail to articulate fundamental questions of the Palestinian people's rights and welfare. The historical examination of the blockade provokes reflections of abiding importance about the impacts of unresolved conflicts and the historical grievances, power relations, and global responsibilities that accompany them. The context provided is important to understanding the extent, validity, and consequences of the blockade. Only then, within that context, can productive discussion be conducted, policy implemented, and mechanisms created for the resolution of conflict and the establishment of enduring peace.

Legal Frameworks and Breaches

The legal documents regarding the blockade of Gaza strike the balance of differing and sometimes opposing elements of international law, humanitarian law, and rules of the sea. The situation in Gaza, particularly regarding the scope of the Fourth Geneva Convention and the UN Convention on the Law of the Sea (UNCLOS), is a source of ongoing critical discussion.

International humanitarian law, especially the Fourth Geneva Convention, requires that Israel, the occupying power, take necessary measures to guarantee the safety and security of the civilian population in the occupied territory, including Gaza. These measures would include the provisioning of necessary supplies, medical services, and other forms of humanitarian assistance. However, Israel's land, sea, and air blockade has fundamentally contravened these protective measures and has created untenable humanitarian conditions for the people of Gaza.

In managing the international blockade, urgent issues of the law of the sea relating to the right of free and open navigation, the right of innocent passage, and the definition of a country's territorial waters arise. The unmanned bordering country takes a *prima facie* view of the law of the sea, as set by UNCLOS, in addressing the international validity of the blockade and the hydrometric restrictions within Gaza's waters. In addition, the systematic and arbitrary attacks on Palestinian fishermen and their boats, which often result in attacks on fishermen, attacks on boats, and the deaths of fishermen, constitute a gross breach of fundamental principles and rules of the law of the sea.

The scale and persistence of breaches in international law regarding the blockade have galvanised condemnation from human rights groups, legal professionals, and international advocates across the political spectrum. Numerous accounts and probes have identified the systematic disregard for obligations and norms of legal civilisation and the urgent necessity for accountability and redress. Moreover, the absence of effective enforcement and the failure of the international community to impose adherence to legally established principles has nourished the appetite for the perennial cycle of impunity and injustice surrounding the blockade, an absence of any law that governs international civilisation.

Understanding the legal aspects of the blockade requires an approach that is far wider than rethinking what we have, as well as a comprehensive reaffirmation of adherence to the existing rule of law. Equally important is the need for a multilateral initiative that includes meaningful engagement, diplomacy, and enforcement to address the fundamental and longstanding legal violations and restore the rights and dignity of the people of Gaza.

Economic Effects concerning Gaza

The blockade and its corresponding restrictions have been devastating for Gaza, and during heavy restrictions on trade, unemployment soared, and widespread poverty seized Gaza. Restricting trade and regional integration, Gaza was almost completely isolated from international trade activities, and this stagnated economic growth greatly. The blockade has significantly restricted access to the fishing industry, resulting in increasingly inaccessible fishing zones. The Israeli military practices and regular intakes of fishing vessels have resulted in decreased fishing productivity and stagnated income, negatively dragging down income and employment rates in Gaza.

Restricted territory access greatly impairs the ability for trade with and access to foreign markets, and critical farming resources and materials, coupled with military devastation to productive farmland, have resulted in a supply choke for internal Gaza farming. Furthermore, the local construction and manufacturing markets heavily rely on the import of machinery and materials, which results in economic diversification and local development being stunted. The blockade has resulted in humanitarian aid dependency due to the skyrocketing unemployment and poverty rates, which have led to economic instability and stunted growth.

The blockade has caused dormant economic activity in Gaza, along with food and service deprivation and food insecurity. The restriction on imports has caused food and medical supply shortages, which have led to increased prices. Poorly managed infrastructural, sanitation, and energy services compound the quality of life issue for the people.

The economic problem has led to negative social and psychological impacts on breadwinners. In addition, the enduring "need to escape reality," coupled with the lack of economic opportunities, has driven many youths towards the pervasiveness of risky job markets abroad. The continuously stalled investment opportunities further hinder one's ability to develop and build a resilient society.

We must address Gaza's blockade to promote regional development and ensure economic stability and prosperity. These impacts can be mitigated by removing trade barriers, supporting community structural change through economic investments, and allowing unrestricted movement of people and goods. In addition, international aid and collaboration are essential for the economic recovery and resilience of Gaza that fosters a more secure future for its people.

Tactics and Methods of Enforcement

Gaza's blockade and the exploitation of Gaza's resources involve numerous tactics and strategies personally orchestrated by Israeli authorities. These strategies are intended to maintain cloistered control, access, and domination over a particular land and its resources, including the sea. Navy patrols and checkpoints monitor and control, some fishing and other sea activities. Such restrictions and control over Gaza's coastal waters make it near impossible for many Palestinians to access and exploit sea-based resources for primary and secondary economic activities. Furthermore, the enforcement of arbitrary barriers, such as requirements for permits and licences, helps to solidify the blockade. The complexity of administrative barriers tends to hinder the efforts of Palestinians to conduct legitimate business activities and aggravates the socio-economic conditions of Gaza. Moreover, the blockade on Gaza's borders and the restriction of imports and exports control the movement of goods and critical resources within Gaza and the surrounding regions. Consequently, it fosters the region's dependence on international aid.

Another prominent method of control includes the use of information barriers and manipulation of the power and infrastructure systems of Gaza. This has an effect on important parts of the economy, such as agriculture, health, and industry. The economy of Gaza, along with its people, lives in a state of confined dependency as a result of intentional and systematic forms of electricity and fuel rationing.

Finally, information control coupled with surveillance techniques provides the means for monitoring and controlling communications and the movement of media and data in Gaza. This helps in the censorship of information and the manipulation of public opinion regarding the blockade and the exploitation of resources. The result is that it incapacitates the Palestinians' ability to articulate objections and pursue advocates for change.

Parallel to these tactics, legal and diplomatic manoeuvres move through various channels to gain approval for the maintenance of the blockade and continued extraction of Gaza's resources. The enforcement of legal instruments and international treaties further deepens the Palestinian's plight and attempts to silence those who dare challenge the status quo.

The full adoption of these methods demonstrates the complexity of the enforcement tactics used by Israel and the planned nature of the obstacle to self-determination and sustainable development for Palestinians. The tactics used in Gaza affect all aspects of life, worsening conditions and denying basic rights.

Having Control Over Resources and Possibly Denying Them

The overarching conflict, and particularly in the area of maritime resources, is of great importance. The planned denial of resources to the Palestinian territories, especially the Gaza Strip, is one of the cornerstones of Israel's geopolitical and economic policies vis-à-vis the area. This chapter attempts to shed light on the complex nature of the rationale behind the denial of natural resources to Palestinians and the intricate management strategies employed.

    The vessel of primary concern addresses resource control and exploitation of the coastline and maritime regions of Palestine and the exploitation thereof. Step by step over the years, varying degrees of restriction have been employed by Israel to diminish the ability of Palestinians to access fisheries, the offshore natural gas deposits, and myriad other valuable sea-related resources. Israel's self-imposed and highly fished bordering sea zones, along with arbitrary restrictions on fishing and other economic activities, have stifled and continue to collapse the coastal communities of Gaza and advance poverty and dependency.

    Strategically, and perhaps more importantly, the major disconnect from the aforementioned physically abusive blockade is the targeting and destruction of critical infrastructure, including, but not limited to, electrical grids, the desalination plants targeted for destruction, and the facilities of wastewater treatment plants. These targeted actions not only hold back the development of Palestine as a region considered to be economically underdeveloped, but also add to a century of over-dependence on aid and perpetual humanitarian support.

With the resource under control, it is the absence of dominant control that grabs attention. In the aforementioned case, Israel maintains a dominant position in legal rulings, defining the rules for the governance and utilisation of the resource. As an example – the over and under permissive legal boundaries to the region in question are manipulated by the defender and advocate of the resource over the equal sustainable socio-ecological access within free Palestine, which only denies the control, is processed, harnessed and controlled. Slowly but certainly, the Palestinian people are and have endured the critical attribute of self-sustenance of population to construct a competitive nation.

Depriving a society of resources has a palpable economic burden, but it also comes with significant environmental consequences that resource denial exacerbates. There is significant ecological damage, as well as reckless over-exploitation of the region's natural resources, which is a direct consequence of the indiscriminate resource exploitation and the absence of appropriate resource management and conservation policies of the Israeli authorities. This situation remains potentially catastrophic for the sustainability of natural resources in the region and the possibility for ecological and environmental rehabilitation and recovery.

Detangling the intricate web of resource denial and management strategies requires a thorough consideration of the legal, international, sociological and ethical elements. Attaining effective progress in the equitable resource which is sustainable and properly managed requires a solid devotion to the equitable recognition and resource management obligations owed to every member of shared society.

Depletion of Resources and Ecological Impacts

The environmental effects and depletion of resources caused by this persistent war and blockade on the Gaza Strip foster the wider humanitarian crisis in the region. Accordingly, the relentless and unregulated Gaza environment takes a heavy toll on the life and health of the people, who are stripped of necessary resources and sustainable development. Inadequate and poorly maintained irrigation systems, considered the backbone of sustainable development, coupled with the dire and unreasonable scarcity of clean water resources, culminate in catastrophic pollution and irrecoverable abuse of the terrestrial and aquatic ecosystem. Given the lack and uncertainty regarding vital health issues, most people residing in the region are once again vulnerable to suffering from waterborne diseases. In such cases, it is imperative that the population and, as with most humanitarian issues, the world is jointly and equally responsible.

The capacity of people to think and improve, as challenged by the blockade, only exacerbates matters by reducing people's ability to think critically. More relevant is that the lack of available construction resources remains one of the most suggested issues. Unfortunately, addressing the major limited access to the regional population, constructing major access to the territorial water resources, and extending the least available water channels, such as ducts, to collect and treat sewage is a significant challenge.

Moreover, the depletion of natural resources has affected the ecological balance and the livelihood of the coastal communities of Gaza. Particularly concerning is the overfishing, which has resulted in the decline of marine species and the disturbance of sensitive marine ecosystems, while the blockade has caused economic desperation. These ecological and depletion threats contribute to food, economic, and regional instability.

The challenges mentioned above require efforts to reduce the impacts of the unresolved conflict and blockade on the environment. Gaza needs international support to stop the suffering of its people and to restore the environment. The conflict mitigation steps, which reduce the conflict and address resource management imbalances, include sustainable water management, waste disposal improvement, marine protected areas, and the effective environment-rehabilitation conflict nexus. Access to general resources and free access to imports of green technology and materials are important enablers of the sustainable environment rehabilitation effort.

To conclude, the conflicts and blockades within the Gaza Strip have caused the depletion of resources and have consequences for the environment too. Both require decisive action and global cooperation. It is only by addressing these issues that the rest of the stakeholders can restore Gaza's ecology and ease the suffering of its people. In doing so, the stakeholders can prepare Gaza and its people for a more sustainable and prosperous future.

International Relations and Humanitarian Issues

The response to humanitarian challenges within Gaza on an international scale has undeniably dominated diplomacy and activist causes. Many countries, along with various international bodies, have shown utmost sympathy towards the cruel humanitarian conditions and appeals made to take quick steps to mitigate the suffering and pain and make humanitarian relief available to the suffering individuals. The United Nations has, for the most part, memorialised the suffering and humanitarian needs of the people of Palestine residing in Gaza and has often given the humanitarian needs of such people special precedence. In addition to that, many international relief organisations, NGOs, and humanitarian workers have made efforts to provide relief to afflicted people who are barred and underresourced. In spite of that, insurmountable obstacles remain, owing to a lack of sufficient humanitarian funds; numerous people in distress fail to receive necessary assistance and services. In addition to that, the developments and evolutions of the humanitarian disaster have increased considerably for people who have to face chronic undernourishment, lack sufficient healthcare, and have inadequate facilities for potable water and sanitation. The international community has always been mindful of the need to maintain human rights to safeguard against the violation of international laws, and in violation of international laws, calls have been made for the protection of civilians, as well as calls for the provision of humanitarian assistance.

To address the fundamental challenges hindering the provision of humanitarian aid and promote sustainable approaches that prioritise community well-being and dignity, dialogues, diplomatic efforts, and multilateral forums have been used in the past and in the present, and it seems they will be used in the future too. Human rights defenders, humanitarian attorneys, and ethical professionals have remained at the forefront of the argument, emphasising that responding to humanitarian crises is both an act of compassion and solidarity, which entails decisive action. Their arguments are still being made internationally to solicit support for humanitarianism and the protection of human rights, regardless of political or geographical challenges. The state of humanitarianism in Gaza is still being developed, and I believe that it is unarguable that the international response to this state is, up to now, the most decisive factor determining the future of the territory. The response is capable of changing policy, enabling resources, or even changing the entire cycle to bring forth a positive transformation. I believe the reasons to address humanitarian issues and alleviate suffering are overwhelmingly clear. Additionally, the common humanitarian goals that advocate for such suffering advocate for an absolute focus and unrelenting effort.

Technological Surveillance and Control Mechanisms

The integration of surveillance systems and control technologies into the maritime domain has been an important part of Israel's strategy to assert dominance and restrict the movement of Palestinian vessels. Israel has established a maritime domain surveillance network using sophisticated radar systems, UAVs, and satellites. These technologies offer real-time monitoring and tracking, which enables rapid detection and interdiction of vessels attempting to enter Israeli-controlled or contested waters. Israel's surveillance capabilities are augmented with hydrophone and sonar systems that provide surveillance of subsurface activities. These systems, siloed with other technologies connected directly to an integrated command and control system, streamline estuary enforcement activities, which in turn facilitate swift and decisive responses to presumed violations or unapproved movements into claimed regions. In addition, Israeli authorities are able to exercise meticulous control over the movements and operations of Palestinian maritime assets through biometric systems, which streamline registration, identification, and movement tracking of fishermen and other maritime workers.

The coercive technological surveillance and control mechanisms are worsened by the addition of communication jamming and interception systems, which constrain the ability of Palestinian vessels to coordinate and communicate. Jamming systems are situated within the broader context of control, suggesting that communication is an integral part of the strategy employed to restrict Palestinian activities at sea. The autonomy and safety of Palestinian operators at sea is undermined by the control of communication systems that are interlaced with the ability to operate vessels. The remote-controlled barriers and other physical obstacles, which are also remote-controlled, at principal entrances to the sea demonstrate the extent to which Israel is willing to go to block Palestinian access to the sea. These systems carry sensor systems and automated response systems, which allow Israel to rapidly respond to unauthorised attempts to gain access to contested waters, thereby enhancing their ability to deny access. The electronic identification and tracking systems which are mounted on Palestinian vessels also extend to constant surveillance and the ability to immobilise the vessels remotely if they stray outside defined territorial or operational limits or engage in other activities that are interpreted as violations. Israel's integrated surveillance and control systems demonstrate their intended and sophisticated dominance over sea spaces, and evidence contemporary relations with Palestinian stakeholders in fishing and other maritime activities as one of control and oppression.

Case Studies: The Stifling of Maritime Industries

The lack of development of maritime industries in Palestinian territories serves as a useful, information-rich case study in the multi-tiered obstacles presented by the systematic blockage of Israel. The Gaza Strip has particularly suffered from the inability to develop maritime businesses, including fishing or even basic port infrastructure. The fishing industry serves as a poignant example, where fishermen are reduced to a sliver of the coastline, partially accessing barren marine environments that do not yield the appropriate catch. The Israeli navy restrictions do not only restrict over double the number of fishermen that there are, but also set entire populations of Palestinians into worsening conditions of poverty – down to the essentials of food. The instruments such as naval patrols and satellite monitoring used to enforce such boundaries create a blanket of intimidation and surveillance that paralyses the development and growth of any maritime venture. Another example is the development of port facilities and the ability to develop and serve trade, since these are in themselves stifling components of growth.

Deliberate restrictions on imports of construction materials and equipment crucial for the improvement of port infrastructures and the movement of vessels and handling of cargoes of vessels are strong barriers that propagate the absence of the Palestinian territories prospering over a centre of international trade. This practice hampers the region's economic self-financing as well as dependence on other countries, thereby worsening the social and economic inequality. These case studies illuminate the captured Palestinian coastal economic zone and the maritime freighting industries. The underdevelopment of such a vital zone that could offer a centre for trade and the proper maritime facilities across the region are most telling of the need to develop strategies that would integrate the overcoming of the growing obstructions to economic progress within the region and to the rest of the world. Pathways for resolution and redress must cover a broader spectrum to include the legal, international, and maritime domains of the proactive measures that could be undertaken to help these industries. Vexatious maritime industries, as demonstrated by the above micro-case studies of economically repressed cases, need a robust, internationally coordinated response caused heavily by the absence of basic friendly international relations.

Pathways to Resolution and Reconciliation

In doing so, the quest for peace and stability in the region requires that we explore the few remaining, but viable, pathways to resolution and reconciliation. The complex socio-political environment in the region dictates that all approaches be sufficiently nuanced and sensitive to the concerns and ambitions of all the parties involved. At the very heart of this quest is the recognition of maritime domain rights and the equitable apportionment of the available resources. Reconciliation is possible and attainable within the framework of international diplomacy and law.

One fundamental pathway requires that all relevant parties be engaged in productive dialogue and negotiation. There are a number of ways, both within direct bilateral collaboration and within diplomacy more generally, to try to help develop mutual trust and understanding. This is what requires relevant and focused discourse that is more than just the negotiation of peace and the redress of historical grievances but a robust mutual vision for a future that is thriving in peace, cooperation, and coexistence.

In addition, the creation of joint economic and resource-sharing projects can also be extremely effective in helping to foster interconnection and interdependence. When integrated economic systems are constructed, relevant parties can help lessen the economic pressures of a zero-sum game approach, thus helping to create a more peaceful environment that is more conducive to reconciliation.

Furthermore, spending time on educational initiatives and

cultural exchanges can close the gaps of empathy and understanding for the younger generation. The foundations of enduring reconciliation can be cultivated by fostering an atmosphere of acceptance and appreciation for differing viewpoints.

The unified support of the international community, which includes major international stakeholders, lends crucial support for the advancement of confidence-building measures and the sustainable peace initiatives which lend regional actors admitted to the international community, which require a regional level of peace.

Track-two diplomacy and people-to-people interactions diplomacy could also be harnessed to inform the channels of cooperation and dialogue. Reconciliation and societal trust-building, which serve to support the leaders at the desk of diplomacy, are also provided by the arms of civil society and local-level movements.

The leadership which, alongside single-minded dedication, also possesses the imagination necessary to foster pathways for the enduring peace sought in resolution is at the centre of the will needed. The region can be their destination, cooperating and harmoniously prospering, provided the narratives which lead them are burdensome are set aside to allow conciliatory efforts to compromise and new collaborative approaches to be embraced.

7
The 2023 Heist
Licensing Foreign Giants in Disputed Waters

Introduction to the Maritime Controversy

Maritime controversies, especially those concerning the ever-growing disputes over territories, have always been some of the hot topics of the recent past. The integration of history, modern jurisdiction, and the economy in these areas seems to generate more disputes and contention than ever over them. Every dispute boils down to the question of territorial sovereignty, the question of resource exploitation, and the equally complicated question of international law. Participants in these disputes and controversies are usually nation states, regional players, and overseas stakeholders fighting over pivotal maritime territory. Such disputed waters are not only elements of tension in modern politics. They are also economically advantageous, rich with hydrocarbon resources and vital maritime pathways. Complex histories, including diverging views of some ancient borders and treaties, only serve to enrich and complicate maritime disputes, in light of hundreds of contradictory claims. The development of international maritime law, along with the application of such instruments as the United Nations Convention on the Law of the Sea (UNCLOS), are also protracted issues, which make these intricacies more complex. They affect the way countries exercise their desires on the seas in terms of the international legal framework.

Knowledge of the different aspects of such controversies at sea is important for grasping their implications on the stability of the region, about energy in the world, the likelihood of conflict, and the ability to resolve such conflicts.

In this regard, the disputes require an exploration of the facts of history, the present territorial claims, and the economic drives underlying the controversies at sea in the many regions of the world under dispute.

Historical Claims and Contemporary Jurisdictions

The types of geographical and legal issues dividing deep-water parts of the sea span across time and antiquity, continuously being tangled with legal ownership and jurisdictional territory issues. The core of the issue stems from the contradictions regarding the interpretation of treaties, the frameworks of several legal domains, and the geopolitical nature of the area. The epoch of such claims spans several centuries. It is a richly woven, complex narrative of treaties, military outcomes, and borders that have changed and evolved. Indeed, claims to ownership of the aforementioned waters have become mired within a complex web of competing stories and adjudicatory frameworks. In addition to such competing claims, the feeble attempts to adjudicate such claims are always complicated by the multitude of contradictory claims to an array of historical chronicles and events that serve to substantiate such claims. In present time, claims to ownership of particular parts of the sea have rapidly expanded because of the reach of advanced technology and the ability to extract resources that were once considered too hard to reach. Resource, land, and security issues have further complicated international relations among a multitude of states and have created deep-seated conflicts within a web of relations. However, as time evolves, so do the approaches and the strategies that are employed to support or counter the historical claims, as well as modern jurisdiction over sea waters. The claustrophobic tensions that surround relations among the stakeholders are further deepened by the unending desire to extract resources from economically profitable disputed waters and over-manoeuvre within the complex frameworks of international relations and legal structures designed to govern waters and Sea parts that are owned or disputed.

While in pursuit of just solutions that would redress historical grievances along with contemporary interests of all stakeholders, inequitable obstacles still remain. These inequitable obstacles require sharp reasoning. These obstacles need keen diplomacy along with a comprehensive grasp of the multifaceted historical assertions and current legalities that accompany them.

Economic Considerations of These Disputed Waters

Geopolitically motivated tensions that continue in these current times have also been focused on the Eastern Mediterranean and the waters directly adjacent to them. These areas are affiliated with natural resources, especially natural hydrocarbon resources, thereby making them important to current times. The energy that can be acquired from these resources can serve as marketable goods. As a global energy supplier, the Eastern Mediterranean is a valuable region and centre of the global energy market, so most energy companies are keen on investments in these areas. The anticipation of rising global energy markets prompts other companies to invest resources in a competitive energy market. The reserves remain untapped and rigid. Moreover, the bottom-line focuses on more than just the possible energy reserves located in the region. As has been previously mentioned, the location offers opportunities linked to trade and development, transportation, and the establishment of trade routes. All these factors have thus increased the economic value and the interest coming from all over the world, whether it be in the region or in the world.

However, the increased economic interest has intensified existing tensions and disputes. Conflicting territorial claims together with overlapping exclusive economic zones have all increased the friction which is already present among states and their territorial claims. The politics which accompany the control over the region have altered the previously existing geopolitical structure, allowing the world to witness a lattice of conflicts and alliances which go beyond just the obtaining of resources.

The aforementioned proclivities are not exclusive to the economically driven world, especially during a time of grievances and overambitious. Contained in the policies implemented by the parties concerned is the region's economic value, which is integrally linked with the political stance of the region and forms the core of the interactions and policies which are put forth in the negotiations. Considering these developments, one of the key questions in appreciating the conflict in the region is the underlying economic interest of the disputed waters. The economic interest has become intertwined with the political interest and geopolitical calculations, demonstrating the complexity of the issues involved. Understanding the economic aspect of the discourse is critical in seeking balanced, domestically and regionally sustainable solutions that address the nexus of wealth in resources, power, and stability of the region.

Maritime Laws Concerning the Disputed Area

The laws of the sea related to the waters in dispute are a mixture of legal, historical, and international diplomatic puzzles. The focused claim of almost all the countries in the region is centred around the idea of territorial waters, which is the region that extends up to 12 nautical miles from the shoreline of a country. Beyond this zone, there is a zone which is termed an exclusive economic zone (EEZ) that can stretch up to 200 nautical miles with permission to explore and exploit the resources. The case of the waters in dispute off Gaza is an example where the question of who has jurisdiction is very sensitive and hotly contested.

While UNCLOS is the most important legal document concerning borders and bordering disputes of the seas, the intricacies of filing port claims under UNCLOS are another issue. Also, the enforcement of UNCLOS tends to become problematic when powerful nations pursue their interests in hotly contested territories.

Conflicting historical claims and the basis of bilateral agreements make the enforcement of maritime laws in the region rather difficult. A case in point is the clash between Israel's claims of dominance over the offshore resources of Gaza and the claims the Palestinians lay over and historically used them. The absence of a boundary freely acknowledged by both sides makes the enforcement of legal rules very problematic and prone to different interpretations.

Apart from UNCLOS, the inclusion of local administrative entities and other international bodies adds another layer to the governance of maritime laws. The geopolitics and legal wraparounds concerning the Eastern Mediterranean become even more complex with the input of bodies like the Arab League and the European Union. Additionally, the different approaches and interpretations of customary international law by different units of the governing structure make the system of enforcement and compliance of maritime laws in contested regions even more complex.

From analysing the interplay of the factors above, it is apparent that governing maritime laws in such contested territories is not an easy task. With changing circumstances, the importance of grasping the legal complexities, the historical background, and the socio-political environment relevant to this issue is bound to intensify. The reality of the situation is that the maritime domain is so complex. The above factors in combination reinforce the need to develop appropriate legal frameworks to deal with such complex cross-border maritime issues.

Licensing Protocols – A Web of Ambiguity and Power

Within the domain of licensing protocols relevant to disputed waters, the assignment of drilling rights, exploration permits, and production-sharing agreements is as complex as a journey through fog and a fierce battle. Balancing the law and the legal, political, and economic frameworks is a difficult balance to strike. At the centre of this battle is figuring out the ownership of and authority over the contested maritime boundaries. The tussle over licensing protocols is made more intense by the struggle over the contested natural resources. The more territory a resource covers, the greater the draw. In light of the above factors, the interweaving strands of politics, geopolitical standards of manoeuvring, and legal and commercial systems create a tension in the entire spectrum of licensing procedures. Each legal clause, each decision, and each contract made in a region has the potential to alter the energy market in that region and bring about geopolitical balance. The more controlled this information is, the more Canada selling energy to other countries will find out about the situation in the other country's market and gain a competitive advantage. With the manipulable and exploitable situation, the more these systems balance Canada, the more energy they will find for sale, and the greater the region will destabilise. What most of these advancements will point to is that the more the centre is abused, the more opaqueness the Portal Guidelines sustain will erode. The more dominant Canada is, the angrier Canadian energy merchants will be. Each of these factors works in a cycle, and the quicker manipulable agreements and strategic frameworks are established, the more energy will be sold in the market.

The Palestinian authorities are also tasked with attempting to navigate deep and twisted policies to gain participation and representation in an area monopolised by heavyweights. The Palestinian authorities' attempts to protect their legitimate interests and rights within the contested waters are compounded by administrative obstacles and the absence of equitable frameworks. The situation on the ground, which on the surface appears to be governed by international rules and standards which are designed to promote justice and fairness in the licensing of activities, gives an impression of an unequal contest dominated by predatory self-interest and geopolitical theatrics. The complexity of licensing, then, is a question that demands appreciation of the legal obscurities, the contours of interlocking and competing power relationships, and the dynamics of interest in the situation. There is little doubt that control, exploration and extraction of petroleum resources within the contested waters – the emerging saga of licensing – when stripped to the essentials, go beyond economic dimensions to a contest of power, control and hegemony replicas interlaced with geopolitical conflicts and dominance in the region. Grasping and untangling this mesh of power and obfuscations is essential to understanding the repercussions and consequences for peace and stability, equity and control that the region's seas hold in peace and stability.

Key Players – The Emergence of Foreign Energy Behemoths

The battle for control over natural resources within contested waters has piqued the interest of some of the greatest companies in the field of energy – dubbed 'foreign energy behemoths'. Such companies have the capital and technological prowess necessary for the large-scale development and extraction of offshore energy reservoirs. Their presence in the global energy market adds to the already fragmented geopolitical and strategic calculations of the stakeholders in such maritime disputes. The presence of foreign energy behemoths in the contested maritime regions presents a paradox of benefits and disadvantages to every stakeholder involved. These companies economically focus on the market and attaining substantial power in an energy sector, and thus command a considerable say in the outcome of such extraction ventures. These companies have the scale and scope of business activities that are supported by complex contract databases, sophisticated exploration systems, and advanced logistical networks. The activities of such companies, especially the legal political boundaries of each nation, increase the area of interest for regulatory bodies, diplomats, and enthusiasts of ecology.

While aligned with particular state objectives, foreign energy corporations deal with a quite high degree of autonomy and independence, at least in part because of their global footprint, which allows them to push their agendas and secure favourable conditions. In this context, these foreign energy corporations' strategic actions and built partnerships can significantly alter the estimates of power in the energy context of a given region and influence diplomacy and the distribution of resources. In addition, the foreign energy corporations' actions in a given region may also contribute to the sharpening of the competitive climate, which can result in aggravating the conflict escalation in the region. Thus, foreign energy corporations' activities in contested areas go beyond the mere economic rationale and complicate the nexus of sovereignty, resources, and international relations. These foreign energy corporations, which operate in contested areas, embody the interests of a country akin to other global actors, and their actions dramatically shape the current state of the contested maritime region.

Israel's Strategic Developments in the Licensing Arena

In the context of the Eastern Mediterranean, the issue of leasing the right to explore and extract the oil and gas resources within the contested and sensitive geopolitical framework of this region has acquired a significant degree of focus in relation to strategic and policy frameworks. In this 'licensing arena', Israel, through a series of defensive and strategic steps, seeks to control the capital invested in the stub (maritime, energy, and resources) and within the bounding frameworks of the disputed territories.

The strategic element of Israel's positioning, which is one of the more critical poles, is to use the political and psychostrategic touchpoints of the alliances and legal domains which would help to consolidate Israel's position. Through bilateral agreements and partnerships with prominent players within the global system, Israel has tried to ensure the legal system of the Gulf waters is pivotal. In relation to court points aligned to overshadow global one-poles, Israel has tried to 'reach to healing wounds' (attaining balance) through the system of geopolitics and oil and gas politico-economics. Moreover, Israel has successfully capitalised on its economic strength and technological innovations to improve its position in the licensing market. Israel has successfully marketed itself as a desirable partner to a number of multinational firms interested in the region due to its demonstrated capabilities in offshore drilling technologies and its marketed ability to generate significant profits as a result. This strategic branding serves to improve foreign interest and further consolidates Israel's reputation as a leading country in the maritime energy industry.

Beyond these blatant actions, Israel has, for a long time, mastered the art of international maritime law and border conflicts to further its licensing ambitions. Supposedly, Israel has masked her actions and decisions pertaining to the distribution of exploration rights in contested waters by using the legal loophole system to her advantage. By judicially constructing the licensing discourse and its surrounding developments, Israel has managed to persuade decision-makers to license a legal gap.

Israel's steps in manoeuvring within the licensing domain go beyond legal and economic boundaries; geostrategic considerations come into play as well. Winning geostrategic outcomes from licensing is important in sustaining Israel's regional dominance and increasing its strategic concentration within the Eastern Mediterranean. Israel seeks to strengthen its strategic posture within the licence regime by acquiring and controlling key energy resource regions. Israel's primary aim is to dominate the energy geopolitics of the region and enhance its strategic geopolitical standing.

Thus, Israel's activities in the licensing domain are illustrative of the geostrategic interrelation of legal, economic, and geopolitical structures. Similarly, the legal, economic, and phenomenal orchestrations are reflective of Israel's intricate and strategic workings interlaced with the document's key ideas. These are indicative of the document's broader regional geopolitical repercussions.

Problems confronting Palestinian Territorial Authorities

Both the context and the scope of Palestinian territorial authorities' interests regarding the waters in dispute present multiple problems. One of the most considerable is the dominance of uneven power relations within the region between Palestine and Israel, which influences every aspect of business and comes from the fact Palestine is in defence. This imbalance may skew the equality of the negotiating table and the deciding power, which Palestinian authorities need to have to reasonably defend their positions. Moreover, the global fact that Palestine is more of a quasi-state is not helpful, and it certainly does not empower Palestinian authorities in international engagements and diplomacy. Consequently, the fragmentation of Palestinian international relations and the absence of what is termed 'rationalised governance of the sea' become the cause of the burdens which confront Palestinian authorities. Less than effective strategies for the allocation and control of sea territorial rights within the boundaries of Palestine render much of the proposed management unexercised, especially control. Additionally, Palestinian authorities in the context of Gaza face multiple problems in the exploitation of their maritime resources due to the closure imposed on Gaza by Israel. The closure has resulted in a lack of access to the required instruments, technology, and personnel, which has made it impossible for Palestinian authorities to fully explore and exploit their maritime territory.

The Palestinian leadership has further difficulties in reaching coherent maritime pattern objectives, not only because of maritime politics. Conflicting interests among Palestinian disparate governance units can cause strategic paralysis at any step in the development and management of maritime frameworks. In sum, the Palestinian authorities are losing in the complicated and contested waters due to multiple and layered challenges that require deft problem-solving to meet the overarching maritime objectives.

International Reactions and Concerns

The dynamic dispute in the Eastern Mediterranean has become the centre of a heated, multi-faceted debate and has given rise to a myriad of concerns, which embassies and international actors are monitoring closely. Prolonged clashes over territorial passages have geostrategic consequences that diplomats in many desks are concerned about.

As it pertains to the Eastern Mediterranean border dispute, European Union states have become increasingly worried about the potential impact of the disproportionate licensing deals. In the absence of any enforcement of peace at the border, the Bloc focuses on maintaining a balance among the disputers and recognising the rights due to all. There is also a distinct emphasis on fostering international relations in the region among Union members. Dialogue and the use of diplomacy to solve differences are highly in demand.

In contrast, the United States has taken a tempered and practical approach, arguing for the need for order and safety in the area. American diplomats have tried to sustain a strategic partnership with Israel while also recognising the legitimate concerns of the Palestinian authorities. At the same time, the U.S. has advocated for reasonable and fair outcomes that serve the interests of all parties involved.

In addition, adjacent states, namely Egypt, Jordan, and Turkey, have paid particular attention to the shifts in the Eastern Mediterranean, aware of the local geopolitical dynamics and the economic possibilities. Each state has defined its interests and issues regarding the maritime conflict, resulting in a dense complex of many overlapping positions and actions to protect national interests and foster regional stability.

Russia and China, in contrast, have emphasised the need to comply with international law and respect the rights of sovereignty in the worsening sea dispute. Both countries have promoted a multilateral approach and diplomatic means to quell the fighting and reach fair proposals that are reasonable and inclusive.

Concerns for the fragile equilibrium of the Eastern Mediterranean region have been widely felt, with the prospect of conflict and instability being especially worrisome from the point of view of global peace and security. Thus, while global society is deeply concerned about these developments, there is apparently a growing readiness for decisive action to prevent the further escalation of the conflicts and to pursue peace through the proper channels of negotiation and the respect of relevant legal principles.

Conclusion: Shifting Dynamics and Future Implications

Now that we have discussed the international reactions and concerns regarding the licensing of foreign giants into contested waters, we are confronted with the need to analyse shifting dynamics and future implications. The stall of the geopolitical landscape requires reflective thought about the probable consequences and various possible outcomes that could stem from these developments.

Shifting Dynamics

The balance of power and influence in the region has certainly been impacted by the presence of foreign energy companies in the disputed maritime territories. This development not only alters primary stakeholders' strategic assessments but also adds additional layers of competition and cooperation. Historical disputes are now being modified by the economic and geopolitical interests of outside actors. This requires a new evaluation of the current approaches.

Regional and international stakeholders will play a crucial role in setting the future course of the dispute. The allocation and exercise of power, along with the collaborations formed, will guide the foreign and internal policies of the state. These policies respond to changes in the region, and the changes in the region respond to the policies set. The policies, region, and changes are all determinants of the area's stability. These changes also reflect on the changes to the livelihoods and aspirations of the local people, a crucial part of the situation that requires attention through the lens of domestic geopolitics.

Future Implications

The consequences of the 2023 heist and the foreign boarding giant's subsequently licensed privileges go far beyond what the current economic advantages or losses may indicate. The resource management, environmental protection, and the form of self-determination might as well be affected. Thus, this is the rationale behind understanding the existing scenarios and the impact they might have given the current state of affairs.

From the perspective of state affairs, these consequences are disproportionate compared to the bilateral and multilateral negotiations required to sort out the demands and claims of the concerned parties. The evolving energy resources of the Eastern Mediterranean raise equally valid concerns about the ethics of resource distribution, cooperative paradigms, and the feasibility of advantage to all parties concerned. The other aspects related to the stability of the region as well as the security dynamics and the attainment of justice are all the more relevant in the context of these consequences.

The end of this conversation still requires monitoring, action, and a nuanced conversation. We need to anticipate ongoing, and in some cases, complex repercussions, which require a multi-faceted, ethically responsible approach that values conversation and dialogue, a willingness to set aside gains that might be immediate and easier, and giving thoughtful attention to that which will be sustainable over the long haul. The lessons captured here will keep the pages of history looking forward to balance, fairness, and lasting peace.

8
Trump's Riviera Dream
Resettlement and Resource Control

Vision of a New Middle East – Unpacking Ambitions

The concept of a new Middle East, updated from its historical context, results from a set of objectives that extend beyond mere politics. It raises the region's history of economics and security by attempting to change its geopolitical reality and the world's geopolitical landscape. The new Middle East is an attempt to transform this region. It rests on the reconfiguration of the new alliances and relations the countries of the region will establish. The ambition is to make this region the central part of economic prosperity and innovation. This ambition extends beyond the bold. It combines domains of diplomacy, trade, technology, culture and people, which is the desired outcome. It encompasses building a network of countries with shared interests and objectives, bound by cooperation. An analysis of the uncharted territories within this proposed paradigm strengthens and reinforces the strategic needs and ulterior objectives of unravelling the region's challenges. The analysis of the region's policy will highlight both the opportunities and challenges that are relevant to its policy objectives.

Foundations of Diplomacy – Strategic Repositioning

As the realignment of the Middle East's geopolitical paradigm takes root, the foundations of diplomacy take on critical roles in repositioning the global paradigm. As stakeholders reposition dependencies and expectations, diplomacy serves as the medium for new partnerships and the transformation of old ones. This chapter explores the complex web of diplomatic realignment and the navigation of strategic changes central to the new vision for the Middle East.

The linchpin of this strategic repositioning is an intricate latticework of historical partnerships, regional geopolitical constellations, and global economic compulsions. States operate in an arena beset by ancient hostilities and changing friendships, striving to attain positions of economic and security leverage. The regional gaps weave together within this tapestry, creating an intricate diplomatic mosaic against simpler geopolitical backdrops.

Diplomacy slowly and carefully alters the outline of alliances, marking the changing landscape of diplomatic activity. Major actors engage in reformulated conversations that seek to reorganise the centre of the world.

Reframed diplomacy involves multilateral forums, bilateral relations, and even private dealings, all of which focus on synthesising a new configuration in the Middle Eastern theatre. The newly established parameters within the arena are primarily focused on ongoing economic diversification and resource consolidation. Nations try to brand their foreign policies to attain vital trade routes, resource-rich countries, and key maritime parts. At the same time, the finer points of energy diplomacy are undergirded by the overarching geopolitical ambitions of the world, which feature resource-laden zones as the subject of spirited diplomacy. Under these circumstances, the core of diplomacy becomes increasingly urgent, with the aim of modernising cooperation and competition in diverse forms within the region. This glimpse acts as the focal point of interest because the aggregative economic considerations, which are geopolitical in nature, are sensitive and carefully balanced, insisting on redefining the elusive nature of diplomacy. In the same way, these pending reshuffle stories in one direction of political realism and geostrategy indecisively challenge the will of a state to tame a drive based on a new order in a region, defending the fusion of aspiration and pragmatism that is eagerly sought after. The regional vision is shifting with every new diplomatic activity and every new geopolitical reorganisation, which is the result of tectonic changes in the balance of power.

During this period of great change, diplomacy emerges as foundational and continues to guide change in the geopolitics of the Middle East while opening up new, never-before-imagined ventures of cooperation between former enemies.

Economic Allure – Envisioning Mediterranean Prosperity

The aspirations of the various stakeholders in Mediterranean Prosperity present both opportunities and challenges. The region, surrounded by the Mediterranean to the south and the oil- and resource-rich nations of the Middle East to the southeast, presents an undeniable potential for the exploitation of natural resources and the revitalisation of valuable trade routes. Unsurpassed opportunities for portable wealth await the Mediterranean. The exploitation of the region's natural resources, along with the Mediterranean's strategic geolocation, beckons the interest of eager market players who want to raise economic activity and stability in a particularly volatile region.

At the core of this "dream" are the anticipated offshore gas deposits and the potential of expanding the domestic energy market, the beginnings of a vibrant energy market, and the expansion of the gas market due to the existence of abundant energy resources to be tapped for export. Envisaged by regional powers, economic diversification is to be attained through investments in modern infrastructure, reinforced transit routes, and streamlined port services, which will facilitate cross-border movement of goods and services.

Likewise, the appeal of Mediterranean prosperity is not purely economic since it entails potential collaboration, comprehension, and relations, with an emphasis on peace, with countries historically plagued with strife and suspicion. The initiative has the potential to enhance regional cooperation by stimulating economic engagement and development.

The pursuit of Mediterranean economic prosperity raises delicate governance and responsible usage of resources and materials, as well as undue pressure on the environment. Development of proper economic policies focused on peace and sustainable growth is critical for the region. These policies, characterised by an unparalleled economic vision, will help prevent uncontrolled, self-centred policies that exacerbate the suffering of people affected by conflict.

The assumption of the economic charm is the complex charm of the region, which is the internal coordination of governance to the estimates of fairness that encompass all parties in the region, flattering the lineage. Additionally, regional and global cooperation ought to be developed to resolve arising imbalances and conflicts and foster fairness and balance in the economic growth.

In light of these considerations, the concept of Mediterranean Prosperity is indeed complex, as it combines economic, geopolitical, and sociocultural factors and emphasises the need to comprehensively and cooperatively pursue the region's inclusive and sustainable prosperity.

Infrastructure and Development – Paving the Way

Provision and management of any region's infrastructure is a pivotal aspect in the region's socio-economic configuration. In the Mediterranean region, where prosperity ambitions merge with geostrategic realignments, the infrastructure concept stretches well beyond the mere physical and logistical borders. It involves a complex of systems and services designed to promote economic and social development and the rational utilisation of a region's resources. The 'new Middle East' vision compels the region's infrastructure and development to be of primary importance. The modern, strong, and interlinked infrastructure going beyond economic purposes is a precondition of peace and stability.

The infrastructure projects on such a broad scale require advanced planning as well as regional knowledge on social, environmental, and economic sustainability. We need to address the balance between these competing and equally important factors. The inspired implementation and construction projects planned for the Mediterranean area offer numerous challenges and opportunities. These challenges and opportunities range from extensive territory planning for urban metastasis, gauges, and port centres; energy conduit systems; digital information network intersections; and border transit systems to a more simplified reevaluation of the entire system of state governance, laws, and the investment system. Using investment for sustainable infrastructural development, innovation, competitiveness, and foreign direct investment (FDI) can be pulled as a positive outcome. A more comprehensive development of integrated systems of transport and logistics can lead to a decrease in socio-economic barriers to trade and promote increased trade and regional integration along with social-economic cohesion. A more comprehensive energy system, along with renewable sources of energy and exploitation of other natural ecosystem resources, can offer possibilities for energy security along with collaboration and mutual advantages.

In this context, assessing the involvement of stakeholders, public-private partnerships (PPP), and other multilayered frameworks is critical. These frameworks and their implemented projects can be valuable for fusing different aims, utilising knowledge, and providing a fair result for a wider layer of the population. These frameworks and projects need to be counterbalanced with self-governance over local disparities in technology, sustainable development frameworks, and educational resources to promote development equality. The design of self-governing systems with mutual accountability is also significant to set boundaries on potential opportunities for deviation such as misallocation, unscrupulous interference, and influence.

To put aspirations into action means that there is a need to pursue new technological advancements and their applications. Investment in intelligent infrastructure, digitalisation, and green technologies will improve operational productivity while promoting environmental sustainability, as well as fostering knowledge-based economies and new jobs. Climate resilience and disaster preparedness programmes, which are protective, proactive measures that safeguard against natural disasters while assuring operational continuity and the safety of lives and livelihoods, are essential.

The Mediterranean fusion of infrastructure and development offers a transformative canvas with great promise and enduring challenges. Constructing a cohesive approach to aspirations, knowledge, and capital will steer this voyage towards development, prosperity, and enduring peace.

Resettlement Policies – Shaping Demographic Realities

Within the context of changing the region's demographics, settlement policies are implemented as a controversial and complex strategy. The concept of resettlement is viewed within the politics, economics, and the dynamics of security, which makes it burdensome.

To the current leadership, resettlement could strategically change the current makeup of the population in a given area. Through the resettlement of the population, the government intends to control the area and thus reinforce the claims while countering the historical demography. The targeted population changes are likely to alter the social and cultural structure of the target area.

At the centre of the resettlement policies is the question of control over territory. Targeted relocation of individuals and communities achieves control over broken population structures. In the case of physical relocation, the aftermath involves a shift in identity and loyalty. The proposed settlements for displaced people will clearly be part of a broader strategy aimed at controlling the territory and shaping its future.

In addition, the conversation on resettlement policies impacts the policies. Ethically, analysing the displaced people on the border necessitates the development of protective frameworks. Any framework to protect people from being displaced requires a very sophisticated human rights strategy that addresses these issues as well as the fundamental rights of those we consider at stake in these matters.

Besides the socio-political dilemmas, resettlement policies align with economic activities and control of resources. The designed control of people relates to the strategy of gaining control of essential resources and trade regions, which increases rivalry and affects the equilibrium of trade. The resultant movement of people is said to change the distribution of population, the arrangement of complex interdependencies of buyers and sellers, the circulation of property, and/or the untangling of the interdependencies of economic control, which shifts the equilibrium of trade.

In the end, the impact of the policies on resettlement is defined by the appraisal of geopolitics, which does not include the policies' framework. Focussing on the essence of population shifts complicates the relationship between regional unrest and changes in cohabitation, survival, interrelations, and the need for balance.

Resource Allocation – Control Through Commerce

While discussion of the unsettled political landscape continues, it's important to note that the allocation of resources is still key to control and influence. Resource management and distribution can serve as control instruments in determining and asserting geopolitical relationships. As in the envisioned case of resettlement and imposition of resource control, it is necessary to explore the ways in which commerce becomes a deep and complex concrete channel of power and authority. Resource allocation, distribution, and control are not just logistical activities – they are tools of governance and political control in conflictual and contested contexts.

Land, water, and energy reserves constitute vital resources, and their control is a part of a wider political geo-economy crossed with territorial designs. Moreover, the control and manipulation of trade and commercial activities serve as means to create dependencies and, therefore, control inter-regional relationships. Resource allocation in this case becomes more and more important as an extension of political power and aspirations to control the region.

In the course of examining the circulation and allocation of resources, it is apparent that control through commerce is not only a question of material benefits but also of control and superiority in the region.

The economic impact of focusing on specific industries and communities is a change in population and socio-economic conditions , as well as the social structure of that area. Furthermore, the natural change in resources can raise some of the environmental problems already present in that area. These problems add to the already complex system of controlling these resources. These problems also raise questions of social justice in terms of access to and control over the development of these resources. It goes on to show the impact of commercially controlling these resources in a region.

To simplify, these control aspects pose an immediate need to understand the roles of private capital, government, and international relations in the system. The overlap of these relations points to the economic and political interests that control the dominance of these resources and alter the lifestyle of the people in the area. The control that a private entity can have over zoning laws and the intent behind these investments influence both the international and local markets. How these resources are allocated to overhead decision centres and the actions that follow demonstrate that there is much more than commerce behind the motives that unite these countries. It's a balance of political and economic dominance that is present.

The impact and balance of these motives needs to be addressed. The slots in the framework must be filled to improve cohesion. These allow for a deeper understanding of the impact of commercial control over the division of resources.

Deciphering the actions and strategies associated with the story of resettlement and the control of resources demands an understanding of the myriad interconnections and the power relations structuring the arrangement of the distribution of resources. In this connection, knowing the complexities and consequences of resource control through trade provides a deep understanding of the geopolitical context and the underlying objectives that drive the transformation of the region.

Diplomatic Ripples – Regional and Global Impacts

Like many examples of resettlement and resource control encapsulated in a 'Riviera Dream', it is not a simple matter to understand and disentangle the weave of local and international diplomatic relations surrounding it. These are, in many respects, 'relevant' to the Israeli-Palestinian issue. These are relevant beyond the Middle East. The Southeastern Mediterranean rests as a cauldron of economic and geopolitical ambitions. It is a diplomatic and stability imperative not only for the direct players but also for the international system. Governance directly touches Lebanon, Syria, Egypt, Cyprus, and Turkey. These are considered 'neighbours' to the area of concern. Their relations are as complex as a structure to hold feathers while a rooster brazenly dips himself into the bonfire. It is derived from a sophisticated interlace and 'system' of power, hostile history, and dependent economies. The conflict is centrally placed around inland sea borders, resources, and territory disputes. The USA, Russia, China, and the European Union, along with other BRICS nations, are likewise globally concerned about the trend. These are particularly active groups of participants who follow trends for economic investments, energy resources, and the geopolitical challenges affecting the Mediterranean region's strategic role in global diplomacy.

Therefore, one could argue that the significance of the 'Riviera Dream' extends far beyond the confines of academic speculation. In fact, those dreams serve to stimulate the international dimension of the 'Riviera Dream' relating to the pressing and complex problems of resettlement and resource management. Any proposed actions or policies will need to be thought out and detailed to reflect the possible and far-reaching international relationships and consequences involved. In addition, diverging interests and views are vital for any proactive diplomacy that seeks to encourage understanding, collaboration, and peace. The conflicts the 'Riviera Dream' creates require complex evaluations of the

'Riviera Dream' along with the historical resentment, the socio-political realities, and even the dreams of the involved parties. The proposed actions, whether through international diplomacy, multilateral initiatives, or asymmetric negotiations, need to consider the cumulative impacts of international relations and the region to provide supportive and equitable results.

Critics and Advocates – Dissecting Public Opinion

In the context of Trump's Dream of the Riviera, public opinions about the proposed resettlement and resource control policies tend to diverge. On one side of the argument, the critics contend that the proposed policies of resettlement are not only unethical but also controversial and akin to displacement, which violates human rights. They also stress social and economic inequality and the social inequities that resettlement-sponsored programs create. In addition, critics argue about the primary motives behind the strategy and control of resources, questioning fundamental fairness and justice. This section analyses in detail the critics and their arguments. Constructing the other side of the argument, the advocates of the plan argue that it is capable of bringing economic development and growth to the area of consideration. They argue that the proposed policies for resettlement, if properly planned and constructed, will help create economically strong and developed settlements. Advocates of the plan also promote resource control and argue that it can generate funds for the development of resources and other initiatives.

To this end, proponents offer examples from other areas where comparable projects have increased the quality of life, as well as the chances for peace. This section, through thematic critique, aims to examine both the support and negative responses, revealing the complexities behind the opposing views. This paper attempts to provide the audience a glimpse of the proposed policies and how public perceptions have divided in light of the arguments and counterarguments made by critics and proponents of the proposals.

Comparative Analysis – Historical Precedents and Parallels

The background of the current territorial and demographic disputes in the region is quite similar. Analysing precedents and parallels in history fosters a better understanding of the complex issues and opportunities that arise from such issues. In having regard to comparable conflicts globally, control over resources and the subsequent population resettlement in most cases is a complex mixture of politics, economy and humanitarian acts. One case is the partition of India in 1947, which was characterised by demographic shifts, bordering conflicts, and the world's largest migrations. This provocation and its resultant conflicts and tensions have shaped the geopolitical outlook of South Asia even today. Another similar case is the world's second postcard, the Korean Peninsula, which is a remnant of the Second World War. Even to this day, it is characterised by tensions and complex negotiations for a split population and confounding territorial control. In history, these cases have been used to demonstrate the negative and protracted effects of displacements and territorial ambitions. In addition, the Balkan Wars of the 1990s offer important lessons regarding the management of ethnonational conflicts and the difficult period of post-conflict reconciliation. The remnants of these wars signify the approach that is required in solving historical issues, as well as the disputes born from claims over resources and land.

Analysing these historical events, we have patterns of displacement and contested sovereignties, along with engineered demographic consequences. Understanding these instances in a broader framework helps us grasp the complexities of the present situation and devise approaches for long-lasting peace and stability. Such comparisons are highly important for policymakers, researchers, and advocacy groups in untangling the complexities of land and resettlement conflict, along with resource control in conflict-affected areas.

Comparative Analysis – Historical Precedents and Parallels

Within the Israeli-Palestinian context, resolving the conflict requires examining the underlying geopolitical, social, and economic characteristics of the region. Current power shifts in international relations and conflict remain determining factors, for which international relations specialists must study. To build any possible future scenarios, one has to analyse the past and contemporary context, the realities of the situation, and the balance of the so-called peace dividend lines and the historical conflict lines. With these variables, one must analyse possible outcomes from the standpoint of decision-making frameworks active in international public law, such as constructivist securitisation and the interests of the engaged international communities.

Lasting peace, as envisioned in the Southwest Asia settlement, has to resolve the social and political relations stemming from the historical emotive, ethnonational attendant to the conflict, settlement of refugees, the allocation and control of vital resources, and the recognition of the state within and beyond the region's scope of interrelated political independence. This control is understood regarding the strategic external interests present in the region and the configuration of internal arrangements, including regional alliances. The democratic peace which stems from the global reflector position of any international conflict settlement resolution is the independence of lines of conflict and hostility.

Equally important to potential peace is the assessment of escalation points and triggers that might aggravate the already existing friction. How the intricacies of the socio-political dynamics of the Palestinian territories, Israel, and rival neighbouring countries shape the contours of war, peace, and diplomacy is vital. Factors like the conflict's changing ideas, people, and economies affect all of the above.

One should not forget that the Israeli-Palestinian conflict and its resolution are only a fraction of the wider implications of the condition of the world. Its consequences are a reference point for the entire region. The global state of affairs, the perception of justice, and the thin threads of peace and coexistence that are likely to break all point to the necessity for a more thriving world. There is also the issue of prospective conflict and peace. This requires a more curious assessment of the situation. Diverse viewpoints should be brought to engage, and lessons learnt from history should be put on the table. We should scrutinise power relations and the incentives given to the actors involved.

After all this, we can still ask a question: How is the prospect of peace looking? Would we define it as disheartening? Perhaps. If so, we should just be ready with fresh diplomatic initiatives that bear the burden of challenges and intricacies and possibilities of wider cooperation, as well as still being easier to reach.

9
Netanyahu's Echo
Ethnic Cleansing and Settlement Ambitions

Historical Context of Israeli Settlements

The roots of Israeli settlements within the West Bank and Gaza Strip date back to the early days of the State of Israel. After the Six-Day War in 1967, Israel began gradually constructing civilian communities intended for Jewish inhabitants in the territories it occupied. The expansion of such settlements was substantiated by an array of factors, including religious, security, and ideological reasons. To some, the settlements served the purpose of reclaiming the biblical lands outlined within the vision of Zionism as Israel. To others, the settlements were integral in maintaining strategic military positions while forming buffer zones to hostile neighbours. Ideologically, the settlements were perceived as the Jewish people's essence, creating them as part of the homeland's historical narrative and centring the notion of the 'redeeming of the land'. Support for settler movements was derived from the notion that Israel needed to strengthen her hold and sovereignty over such disputed territories. The underpinnings of these motives showcased historical, cultural, and geopolitical considerations. The settlements hereto have served to shape and influence the regional conflict, peace deals, and international relations of the state of Israel.

With the expansion of settlements came the debate regarding their legality, impact on the Palestinian people, and consequences for a plausible two-state solution. In relation to settlements, these issues are a part of the larger Israeli-Palestinian context. To grasp the history and development of Israeli settlements and their intricate connections to the conflict, it is essential to understand these complicated issues. Throughout history, people have struggled to integrate different perspectives and goals into a more cohesive understanding, these settlements being a prime example.

Defining Ethnic Cleansing – A Controversial Terminology

Defining ethnic cleansing is not an easy task, especially when it requires considering the controversy surrounding Israel and Palestine concerning the origin of the word while also being aligned to its use. 'Ethnic cleansing' was first used in the 1990s Balkan Wars and often suggests the removal and violent human treatment of an ethnic group dwelling within the borders of a particular region. Another issue is the disproportionate violence inflicted on the local populations of Israel, including the occupied territories of Palestine, and the question of what precisely can or cannot be called cleansing. Just this particular use of ethnic cleansing in the Israel-Palestine context raises profound and often heated controversy. Describing ethnic cleansing in the actions of the Israeli governmental system is subject to a lot of debate, and ethnonational communalists often argue it shows the sheer intent to carry out Palestinian ethnic cleansing. Such people demand the harshest condemnation on humanitarian and legal grounds and call out the prisons, walls, and deportations. On the other side, many people believe this perspective on it is too harsh and does not consider the more practical aspects of the issue. Advocates of these types of policies, often called settlement policies, seek to defend and rationalise the policies because of 'legitimate state interests'. Those interests, as they put it, in the particular settlement case being discussed, appear to be 'defensive'.

The actions taken, they claim, taken together amount to a strategy to isolate and remove the native Palestinian citizens, thus satisfying the definition of ethnic cleansing. Detractors, on the other hand, argue that the reality is more complex and, in many ways, richer than the term suggests, and that the history, politics, and sociology involved are far more intricate. In their opinion, issues such as the concern for security, the historical claim of the Jews to the land, and the contention over real estate add to a reality that is far more complex than the term ethnic cleansing. The discussions over the use of the term 'ethnic cleansing' showcase the ever-so-polarised stances on the Israeli-Palestinian conflict and the lack of a unified approach for dialogue and resolution. As we approach this entire topic that is so crucial and so sensitive, we are required to apply the most tactful and authentic approaches, be open to a range of viewpoints, and understand that narratives shaped with such words impact policy and decision-making profoundly and directly.

Strategic Expansion – Unveiling Settlement Goals

Israeli settlements in the West Bank and their strategic expansion have been a controversial and complex issue all over the world. The objectives of such strategic expansion have changed and evolved over the years while still retaining their political, religious, and security facets. To truly understand the strategic motivations behind these settlements, we must understand the history and the current political state of the world.

To begin with, expansion is fuelled by political motives. The primary aim is to extend control over critical and strategic regions of the West Bank. Israel wants to control these regions to have a physical, demographic, and economic foothold. Specially designed settlements help alter the geography and the demographics of the territory in favour of Israel. With the help of these settlements, Israel aims to change the ground reality to ensure the absence of a Palestinian state in the future.

In addition, strategic expansion advances Israel's security objectives. The settlements are constructed along primary roads and on high ground and help reinforce the military buffer. Control of these critical and strategic areas enhances Israel's defensive capabilities and helps in the projection of military power in the region.

From an economic perspective, the aim of developing settlements is encouraging Jewish economic activities and growth in the region. This involves the construction of infrastructure, the establishment of businesses, and agricultural activities that promote and sustain Jewish settlements. This economic aspect is part of a larger plan to physically and economically integrate these territories with Israel to tighten Israel's control over the areas.

The settlements also hold significant political importance that should not be overlooked. They represent Israel's declaration of sovereignty and control over the contested territories, reconfiguring the political landscape and complicating negotiations and peace efforts. Through the expansion of settlements, Israel seeks to push the boundaries of internationally recognised territories and redundantly assert its control over the region, thus contravening the claimed illegalities as set by the international community.

The unethical and illegal strategic expansions of settlements pose ethical, legal, and humanitarian concerns. They cause displacement, dispossession, and obstructions to the Palestinian right to freedom of movement. Moreover, they cause disputes over the provision and control of land, resources, and water, thus inflaming an already inflammatory situation.

The propensity for strategic expansion of settlers poses critical political, economic, and security challenges as it inhibits peace, stability, and the scope for a viable two-state solution. Setting and implementing evidence-based policies and practices aimed at the roots of settlers' aggression poses an absolute prerequisite for progressing the resolution of the Israeli-Palestinian conflict.

Legal and International Responses

The international community has understood and scrutinised the phenomenon of Israeli settlements on occupied Palestinian territories, as well as the legal issues that arise from them, ever since. The development and proliferation of these settlements have become matters of international concern, prompting various legal and diplomatic measures in an attempt to resolve issues surrounding the settlements and the peace process. Legally, the Fourth Geneva Convention asserts that an occupying power may not transfer parts of its own civilian population to the territory it occupies. Along with various other international legal documents, these conventions form the fundamental framework to assess the legality of Israeli settlements in the West Bank, East Jerusalem, and the Golan Heights. United Nations Security Council Resolutions, including Resolution 2334, affirm the settlements to be illegal and call for a cessation of them, which has been supported by other members of the United Nations as well. Furthermore, the International Court of Justice has offered an advisory opinion on the construction of the wall in the West Bank which reflects the legal obligation of unilateral adherence of every state to international humanitarian law, regarding Israel as a deliberate guarantor. These legal statements represent a strong consensus among the international community on the illegal status of the Israeli settlements.

The scope of international diplomatic initiatives concerning the problem of settlements has garnered considerable international support. Many countries have condemned Israeli settlements and advocated for a just negotiated resolution to the Israeli-Palestinian conflict. Human rights violations linked to the settlements, along with demands for accountability for the violations, have gained support at both international and some domestic levels. Human rights advocates and civil society have been a driving force internationally, aiming to hold Israel's settlement policies accountable. Some international organisations, including the International Criminal Court, have initiated investigations, and in some cases, trials, into potential war crimes related to the settlements. The evidence points to settlements and the legal dilemmas surrounding them. The legal and international approaches regarding Israeli settlements are indicative of the various efforts being made to address this issue. The connection between legal frameworks, diplomatic action, and the responsibility to uphold international law while promoting peace in the region lies within reach of those who wish to resolve the issue.

Policies Under Netanyahu's Leadership

For Netanyahu, expanding settler colonies aligns with his core political goals and serves to justify the support he receives from far-right political factions in Israel. In breach of international law and United Nations' resolutions, the expansion and establishment of new colonies and settlements became a hallmark of Netanyahu's premiership. The noticeable international backlash did not prevent Netanyahu's administration from consistently planning the long-term colonisation of new territories for political purposes.

Previous cabinets also took similar actions, but the current cabinet actively supports and formalises the policy of expanding Israeli settlements, which extends Israeli control over occupied territory. Amid international backlash and legally contested claims of Netanyahu, there has been expansion of targeted Israeli colonial settlements and consolidation of territories occupied.

During this supported colonisation, Netanyahu's government helped build more settlements and homes, and encouraged Israeli citizens to move there with financial incentives. Such politically embraced policies justified the sentiments that rationalised the targeted imposition of peace by the Israeli state, which is required for essential purposes.

Under Netanyahu's regime, the government's initiatives have focused on legitimising and normalising the integration of settlements in the West Bank. These include legalising unauthorised outposts retroactively and extending Israeli civil law into these areas, strengthening Israeli domination and further neglecting the rights of the Palestinians. Netanyahu's policies continue to build on the ruin of any remaining possibilities of a genuine two-state settlement and the dispossession and disposability of Palestinian peoples.

The implications of his policies on the ground are severe. Israeli policies have provoked land confiscation, restrictions of movement, and territorial fragmentation, impacting the social, economic, and psychological wellbeing of Palestinian peoples. The expanded settlements have further affected the profitability of Palestinian livelihoods, leading to increased violence and a rise in both the number and intensity of incidents in the Israeli-Palestinian conflict.

International challenges to settlement policies persist, with diminishing attempts at justified critique. The resultant dispossession, injustice, and inequality of the policies between peoples further deepens the Israeli-Palestinian conflict. The enactment of policies that hinder the development of a genuine two-state settlement keeps the peacemaking discourse solely focused on Netanyahu. The peacemaking inequities towards Palestinians are the fruit of his policies and remain a fundamental point of focus for the conflict overall.

Impact on Palestinian Communities

The activities of Israeli settlers concerning Palestinian communities have been impactful and worrying. These settlements have caused Palestinian territorial losses, strained resource accessibility, and helped stall economic growth. Many settlements are built on exploited Palestinian territory, which ends up shattering and displacing whole Palestinian communities. Their settlements have created dire social and economic problems and hardships for those Palestinians who have had to live in their immediate vicinity. Barriers and checkpoints have worsened mobility and have created great hardships in reaching work, education, and health services. The construction and development of those settlements have cut the open countryside, in turn disrupting the agriculture (farmlands) and the ecology. The living conditions of the Palestinian settlements have thus suffered the most and have led to increased conflicts and tensions in the area. Furthermore, in the area of military rule, the Palestinian residents have been subjected to arbitrary arrests, detention, and unreasonable violence, which has violated the human rights of the citizens. The constant presence of surveillance amplifies the situation and leads to increased stress and trauma, which are already predominant in the communities.

Settlements have altered social relations and other cultural aspects, which have greatly affected the Palestinian way of life. This is a loss of identity and heritage that senselessly threatens the well-being of entire future generations. Palestinian communities, however, have managed to remain resilient and steadfast despite so many obstacles in their way and have fought to defend their rights and heritage. Advocacy of the communities under discussion, coupled with international support, has attempted to defend and promote the rights and dignity of these people. The settlements are the Palestinian people's challenge, and those who advocate for their well-being address this challenge in the context of agency and historical deprivation of it, offering a comprehensive framework which seeks to restore their well-being.

Voices of Opposition – Internal and External Critiques

The controversy surrounding Israeli settlements and concerns relating to their impact on Palestinian communities have historically attracted mainstream attention from both internal and external perspectives. Internally in Israel, there are individuals and organisations who have been oppositional and vocal about the expansion of settlements. These voices of dissent advocate more conciliatory policies concerning the Palestinian territories and argue that any realistic solution has to be fully sustainable for both Israelis and Palestinians.

At the same time, external criticisms emanating from the global community and a number of prominent organisations on human rights, as well as some governments, have highlighted the adverse impact of Israeli settlement policies on the prospects of peace as well as on the Palestinian population. These criticisms also pertain to the violation of international law and, more specifically, the illegal settlement policies concerning the Fourth Geneva Convention that forbids the movement of people from the territory of the occupying state to the territory occupied.

Furthermore, these voices of opposition point out the social, political, and humanitarian consequences of the expansion of the settlements, including confiscated land, constrained movement, and the social and economic inequity between the Israeli settler and native Palestinian populations. In addition, they criticise the protective and proactive violent measures used to advance the construction of the settlements, which increase tensions and reduce the chances of national reconciliation.

It is important to note that these voices of opposition come from different backgrounds and include the political, legal, cultural, and academic circles. Several scholars, activists, and public intellectuals have framed the critique of the settlement policies, offering research and analysis that underpin their arguments and provide fresh approaches on how to achieve a just and lasting peace in the region.

In the context of settlements, such internal and external critiques add to the already rich discourse on the ethical and practical aspects of that issue. They emphasise the need to strike a balance between political actions, fundamental rights, and the potential for peaceful cohabitation. It is imperative to have these conversations and consider these voices to have a better handle on the constructive and destructive aspects of these activities to address peace and stability within the region.

Settlement economy: incentivising growth and sustainability

The settlement economy in the occupied Palestinian territories has generated considerable debate and criticism. Supporters claim the settlements foster economic growth and sustainability for surrounding communities, while opponents denounce them as illegal, immoral, and harmful to the prospects of peace. Compounding the complexities of the settlement economy are the political, security, and peace considerations related to its development.

Proponents of the settlement economy claim it serves to incentivise regional growth. Supporters argue that the development of settlements creates industrial zones, agricultural enterprises, and residential areas that lead to the creation of jobs and the generation of economic activity. Furthermore, advocates claim that settlements draw capital and trigger the development of economically productive infrastructure in the region.

Advocates also argue that the settlement economy offers considerable potential for economic sustainability. They claim that the economic exploitation of the territories' land and water resources offers the region the prospects of self-sufficiency and reduced reliance on external regions. This would, in the advocates' opinion, foster the resilience and economic prosperity of the local people, which refers to the long-term stability of the region.

Yet, critics contend that all such progress occurs at a cost, as settlements extend the borders of the state and boost the economy. Critics point to the unregulated and unrestrained extraction and exploitation of the region's natural resources, often high with negative social and environmental impacts. It is also argued that the discriminatory manner in which resources and economic opportunities are allocated and distributed within the settlements siloed the opportunities and the avenues available in the settlements, and the settlements produced inequalities in the region while impeding prospective inclusive economic development.

The previous critique describes the morally problematic juxtaposition of growth and sustainability in the settlement economy. The well-being and rights of the displaced and occupied indigenous Palestinian population are present but also unsettling. The justified growth occurs within an unsustainable and inequitable economic structure that primarily aims to strengthen the occupation of the land. Critics describe this growth system as an inequitable economic model that also highlights the unsustainability of economic growth within its confined structure.

As a result, complex questions about the settlement economy and its potential benefits for growth and sustainability remain unresolved. Answering these questions requires a detailed analysis of the economic, social, and political factors involved in the occupied territories and the interpersonal and broader questions of the pursuit of peace and justice in the region.

Future Projections and Policy Directions

"The future projections and policies that could provide a sustainable solution to the intertwined issues of Israeli settlements and Palestinian rights are essential. The geopolitical state of the world, and more importantly the region, calls for addressing settlement advancements and their repercussions. One of the future projections is the presence of ground realities and crucial shifts in the socio-political arena. Such information should help policymakers design practical policies that seek to address the wishes and concerns of the Israeli settlers and the Palestinians. Any policy has to start with the principles of international law. It is essential to reclaim the principles of justice and, more importantly, equality. This calls for a change to the established policies on settlements and the bounded territories to settle.

In addition, any new approach should encourage understanding and cooperative initiatives that help promote human rights and dignity for all people impacted by the protracted conflict. Future policy approaches will place a premium on accountability and transparency in the establishment of monitoring, reporting, and verification mechanisms to maintain the rule of law and prevent any actions that could jeopardise the prospects for justice and enduring peace.

An essential part of forecasting the future is focused dialogue and negotiations to arrive at an acceptable and lasting solution. This requires all parties to undertake negotiations with the intention of creating an atmosphere of constructive cooperation. Lastly, the emphasis placed on the need for diplomacy at all levels is a salient acknowledgement of the importance of collaborative diplomacy on the future of policy. Collective diplomacy, from global and regional actors to local constituents, may help identify creative means and advance inclusive strategies. Solutions that are people-orientated may emerge from synergy between policy and policy implementation aimed at equity. A lasting equitable regime that bolsters the peace, prosperity, and well-being of all stakeholders seeking a fair and enduring solution is possible.

Integrating Peace Initiatives with Reality

Leaning towards peace in the Israeli-Palestinian conflict is a challenging endeavour that requires insightful diplomacy and an understanding of the realities on the ground. The planned peace efforts can encompass all the initiatives, but the success of these coordinated efforts is determined by the socio-political and regional realignment of the proposed initiatives.

Within the context of settlement expansion and long-standing tensions, an Israeli-Palestinian peace framework must focus on the issues of sovereignty over land, control over resources, and the rights of the Palestinian people. Grounding the initiatives in the reality of the conflict means addressing the core issues of land, resources, and the needs of the Israeli and Palestinian people. The fears, hopes, and grievances of each side must be acknowledged; there are historical and contemporary antagonisms that need to be reconciled.

Critical to this integration is the idea of trust and the necessity of confidence-building between the opposing parties. Disinterested mediators can provide an arena for the parties to resolve trust issues and construct a framework that facilitates the negotiation of a shared future. What the process requires is a willingness to engage in dialogue on recognition, acknowledging the troubling issues of the past, and politically agreeing to the vision of peace and partnership.

The quest for sustainable peace must also consider the region's economic dependencies. Development programs that incorporate inclusive growth with cross-border economic partnerships can help build relationships between communities while weakening the pull of extremist ideologies. By strategically repositioning economic progress in relation to the dividends of peace, we can motivate the stakeholders to enter economically beneficial cooperative agreements.

At the same time, a significant part of the global community, which includes all international stakeholders, has the unique responsibility of providing the political will, finance, and security guarantees that undergird the possible success of the peace proposals. The effective promotion of peace necessitates an integrated approach that respects international law and UN resolutions and adheres to human rights demands.

Likewise, the restless consequences of rooted historical inequities demand and deserve restorative justice initiatives. Understanding and acknowledging the suffering of both the Israeli and Palestinian peoples will help build the essential foundations for a just and lasting peace.

To fully align reality with peace initiatives, one requires a comprehensive reconceptualisation of the present conditions. This involves a movement away from inflexible zero-sum attitudes to inclusive, rights-based attitudes that recognise the dignity and self-determination of all stakeholders. Lasting peace will take root and grow only within such a transformative framework.

10
The Mediterranean Bonanza
Regional Resources and Palestinian Exclusion

Historical Context: The Geopolitics of the Mediterranean

The geopolitics of the Mediterranean region span across centuries of conflict, strategising, and rivalry, which still continue today. The Mediterranean region, which serves as a connection between Europe, Asia, and Africa, has always been a target of lust for empires that want to capture wealth through trade and abundant natural resources. It has always been a reason for conflict and wealth for empires spanning from the Ancient Greek and Roman civilisations to the Ottomans and Habsburgs.

Power struggles often stem from ancient conflicts revolving around access to fertile lands, valuable minerals, and strategically important ports. The control of maritime trade routes also meant dominance in global trade, which facilitated military influence, leading to massive waves of colonisation and supremacy. The history of the world tells a vivid story regarding conflicts over control and resources, which sanitise the world today.

The Mediterranean region has been a spectacular centre of debate for modern nation-states for a long time, trying to acquire energy reserves, fish, and defend essential trade routes. Hydrocarbons and the offshore oil drilling that developed in the region have heightened geopolitical rivalry and transformed associations along the Mediterranean coast. Oil has been a significant compounding factor hidden beneath the waves.

One particularly contentious issue among strategic peers

is the suppression of wild competition, making the acquisition of oil reserves a sovereign matter. This leads to disputes that can view the entire region as a blank canvas of dubious power. The clamouring of each nation for strategic as well as economic dominance in the world is only enhanced by the state of the Mediterranean.

This has resulted in the Mediterranean region emerging as a competitive field between the two to draw the rest of the world into global trade, ensuring that the Mediterranean continues to be the stronghold of oil reserves and trade in the world. Understanding this modern situation requires being well-versed in constitutional geopolitics and the cultivation of oil reserves around the Mediterranean.

The Riches Below: Overview of Regional Natural Resources

The Eastern Mediterranean's natural resources include offshore gas fields and rich marine life. Hydrocarbons found in the Levant Basin have sparked significant interest in this area and abroad. This has become a turning point in the development of energy resources and economics of Mediterranean bordering countries. Central to these resources are the natural gas deposits found mostly in the Levant Basin and the Nile Delta Basin. The region also comprises oil and even more valuable undiscovered reserves. The Mediterranean region plays an essential role in the geopolitical order, with high-demand resources and rich deposits of oil and gas on the surface and beneath the soil. The Mediterranean is also rich in biologically diverse ecosystems with fish and coral reefs and supports the tourism industry.

Furthermore, the region has massive mineral deposits such as phosphates, iron ore, and other high-value minerals, the utilisation of which could substantially benefit the local and global economy. There is an escalating race to capture such resources, and with it comes the myriad of challenges for their extraction and management. There is a need to balance the quest for extraction with the obligation to protect the environment and promote sustainable development. There are environmental threats from offshore drilling, such as oil spills and destruction of ecosystems, which only highlight the need for controlled management of the resources. Additionally, the distribution of the gains that come from the extraction of resources is controversial, especially today with territorial disputes and the historical background of the region. These problems are not unique to the region. External elements such as other countries' economic interests, environmental needs, and geopolitical rivalries lead to modifications of the challenge, without diminishing its essence as a region. All of these factors are crucial and create a broad policy deficit, which also lacks a regional Mediterranean perspective. Understanding the resources in their full breadth is an important step to fostering cooperation for these comprehensive implications.

Stakeholders and Claims: Navigating Territorial Disputes

The rich and varied natural resources in and around the Mediterranean have triggered serious territorial disputes within the region. As the teams of competing nations and stakeholders attempt to assert claims to the rich offshore gas deposits in these waters, the world witnesses the sharpening of claims and boundaries. Behind all these dominant issues, unresolved disputes relating to the seas and those which are historical, political or economic still prevail. Attempts made by nations to stake their claims, identify their interests, and pursue them in a long and endless struggle have never been easy. This part of the paper will focus on the Mediterranean claims and the complex system of actors involved in the intricate and tangled disputes imposed upon them. There are many countries and claimants to the seabed resources in the eastern Mediterranean as well as the Levant Basin, such as Israel, Palestine, Cyprus, Turkey, Greece, and Egypt. The interests of each of these nations are based on their historical and geopolitical as well as economic connections and interests, which colour the waters of the region to the limits of a near impenetrable web. The complexities of the unresolved disputes are complicated by the inadequacy of boundaries that are agreed upon at a universal level and the competing areas of maritime domination. The lack of agreements in the field of maritime law only adds more heat to a very cool region lacking dispute. The enforcement of indigenous rights, coupled with international law, and the enforcement of diplomacy serve as the backbone of resolving these complicated conflicts. It is equally important to accept the claims of the concerned parties while allocating resources in a fair and just manner. The resolution of the disputes requires a mastery of the art and science of diplomacy, compliance with international law, and a desire to reach a peaceful settlement. The relations of the actors in the territorial disputes in the Mediterranean need to be analysed to reveal the more profound problems of resource exploitation in the region and the resultant access and ownership complications. An in-depth analysis of these problems will highlight the interrelations of the region concerning power, rights, and responsibilities.

Stakeholders and Claims: Navigating Territorial Disputes

Under international humanitarian law, Palestinians are entitled to freely access and utilise the resources of the Palestinian Territory and the resources in the Mediterranean Sea. However, the policies of the Israeli State have effectively and purposefully excluded Palestinians from access to and the ability to utilise the resources along the Mediterranean coast. These access barriers are complex and multilayered, ranging from domain governance and sociopolitical systems to frameworks of law and the continuum of democratic governance. Central to this apartheid exclusion is the Israeli occupation and control of the west of the Jordan River and the absence of functional Palestinian sovereignty. The situation is made even more acute by the denial of justice and the ability of other nation-states to exploit these resources unaccountably and unchallenged to the Palestinian people. The unrestricted apartheid control of the licensing scheme, along with the investment and the exclusionary development at the borders of other nation-states, crosses the development and investment frontiers, resting with the people of these border nation-states, and the indignation and resentment of these communities towards the Palestinian people remains. The lack of democratic control of the people in these regions, accompanied by infrastructure deficits, lies in the absence of investment for the people of these regions.

All these barriers combine to foster and sustain acute disparities in economy and employment, lack of development opportunities, and stark economic feminisation in Palestinian communities.

Moreover, the absence of these elements greatly diminishes the economic self-determination and growth potential of the Palestinian people. Ethically and strategically, as with the Palestinians, ensuring access requires a multidisciplinary approach that is political, legal and economic. This entails advocacy for Palestinian rights and sovereignty, contesting a regime of discrimination and exclusion, and pursuing policies that facilitate the active participation of Palestinians in the stewardship and use of regional resources. Such practices aim to promote active governance, just allocation of resources, and guarantee the rights of all stakeholders in the Mediterranean region in ensuring equity in participation and in the just distribution of benefits. This requires concerted action by international organisations, the state, civil society, and business in advocating for the removal of barriers and the inclusive and equitable resource allocation paradigm. As the Mediterranean region is a collection of systems of intricate exclusion and disregard for the self-determined sustainable development of border and marginalised peoples of the region, the region is also rich in transformational potential and untapped resources that, if unleashed, will lead to justice, equity, and sustainability for all.

Legal Battles: UNCLOS and Beyond

Legal disputes at sea are intricate and comprehensive, as

illustrated in the Mediterranean region. The United Nations Convention on the Law of the Sea, or UNCLOS, serves as the juridical central figure of conflicting maritime claims and maritime boundary setting. During the application of UNCLOS concerning the region's resources, the exclusion of Palestine creates another set of problems. Every legal conflict pivots on the core issues of sovereignty, territorial waters, and the use of cobalt and other resources. UNCLOS offers legal grounds for the declaration of exclusive economic zones, as well as for the rights to the continental shelf; however, the disputes surrounding them are of a substantial nature. The case of Palestine lacks statehood, which creates additional issues, such as the ability to claim and resolve maritime disputes set before the participants in the United Nations Convention on the Law of the Sea. Other complications arise from the geopolitical and international interests and actors, which, along with other elements of international sea law, intertwine and present further complications to the matters at hand. Apart from the United Nations Convention on the Law of the Sea, the pertinent legal issue encompasses broader international law, as well as international customary law.

The Palestinian exclusion, alongside the engagement with all the relevant adversaries in the context of international diplomacy, warrants justice through the use of international arbitration and systemic legal advocacy. Capturing all the battles that are within and beyond the boundaries of UNCLOS readily highlights the intricate framework of unresolved injustices, disproportionate powers, cautious legal geopolitics, and all the overarching ethos of international law. Understanding all the details of these battles provides significant insight into the regional resource context and the consequences of the rational integration of regional resources with Palestinian inclusion and fair rational integration.

Economic Disparities: Wealth Distribution and Regional Economies

Like many regions around the world, the Mediterranean poses unique and complicated challenges regarding the distribution of wealth as well as the regional economic dynamics at play. An example of economic development disparity is the unequal benefits that different stakeholders receive when they claim the wealth located beneath the waters. Economically, the region as a whole suffers when the resources available are not shared equitably.

The disparity in the region results from an intersection of multiple economic, political, and social factors. Gas and other marine resources claim a portion of the wealth and, at the same time, enjoy the mineral benefits, while other portions of the population are relegated to denial of access to their share. Economic terrains are adverse, and the contrasting suspensive conditions give rise to grievances that aggravate tension and fuel friction among various constituencies.

The few politically and economically unified influences that garner the resources further aggravate the situation by predisposing the region and population to top-echelon social systems disguised as democracy. The rest of the population remains economically stagnant and impoverished as the few enjoy the privilege of bounty received from resource extraction. Social development and security become opportunities for exploitation by all the aforementioned factors in the region. These disparities obstruct sustainable development and maintain social and political inequities, hindering the capacity for amicable cohabitation and collaboration.

Examining the regional economies affected by these disparities reveals that the distribution of resources determines the economic trajectory of the countries and regions involved, highlighting that the existing disparities are a significant concern given the abundance of resources in the world that could be utilised and distributed to benefit everyone.

Moreover, the unequal economic benefits resulting from the region's resources affect the economic stability of the region as a whole. They prevent the possibility of creating a cohesive economic region that works on the principle of mutual benefit and shared prosperity. Instead, they create competition and conflict, which restrict the possibility of collaborative initiatives that promote sustainable growth in the entire region.

To mitigate these economic inequalities and promote inclusive regional economies, it is necessary to rethink current resource distribution practices and shift towards collaborative approaches that ensure active participation and equitable resource distribution. This change must be guided by the concepts of openness, responsibility, and inclusiveness with a keen focus on the social and economic conditions of the relevant peoples. This approach would allow change to happen and help eliminate the existing disparities and strive to create balanced regional economies. This process has the potential to transform the entire Mediterranean region into a model of collaborative sustainable growth, mutualism, and shared wealth.

Environmental Concerns: Extracting Resources Responsibly

There are many resource extraction environmental issues regarding the Mediterranean region requiring attention. The issues relating to the vicinity do pertain to land and ocean ecosystems. However, the issues are more wide-ranging because they also involve climate change and international diplomacy.

The extraction of polymers, oils, and gases, along with the exploration and mining of minerals, can lead to various impacts such as habitat destruction, ecosystem contamination, and disruption of the delicate relationships within these ecosystems. The impacts are many, since ecosystems are interrelated and biodiverse. We must also consider the people who depend on the region's ecosystems and the sea for their livelihoods.

The higher carbon emissions added to the atmosphere come from burning oil to fuel machines required to extract the resource. The overreliance and reckless reliance on gas also add to the carbon footprint, increasing climate change effects. There is the non-ignorable fact that negative effects can be communal. One person does not have to bear the environmental issues; on the contrary, many people can bear them broadly.

Palestinians possess no such rights. The exclusion of resource extraction is not the only environmental concern that needs to be addressed. Without adequate extraction, none of these issues will find resolution. The negative impacts, which are likely to be disproportionate, unified and polarised regarding the resource and environmental benefits and protection, are likely to be.

To tackle these complex obstacles, responsible resource withdrawal has to be undertaken. This involves using advanced resource extraction techniques that strive to work within minimum disruption thresholds in the biosphere and fulfilling resource withdrawal prerequisites, such as conducting proper impact assessment investigations. Other than these, active and open communication regarding resource extraction impact and rationale with the Palestinian Authority and the very communities that will be personally affected is of utmost importance. They contend that understanding the negative impacts is crucial, as the world's biosphere is a shared heritage of mankind.

In supporting arguments about the impact of resource extraction that are geared towards minimalistic disruption to the biospheric biosphere, principles that have already been established, such as the United Nations Convention on the Law of the Sea, can help defenders of resource extraction impact go beyond the feedback of the Palestinian Authority to formulate better frameworks that even regional actors can embrace to practise resource management responsibility and protect the biosphere without undue harm.

Allocating funding towards the world's traditional energy, especially coal, will enable these improvements to happen relatively seamlessly. United Nations principles address the world's legendary biosphere to deter negative impacts of resource extraction and support the positive impacts. Embracing these principles can enable the Mediterranean region to further deter adverse impacts without economic development and energy security.

In the end, the meticulous extraction of local resources

balances with resource responsibility, social equity, climate change, and environmental protection. While the Mediterranean resources have always been complicated by the diverse obstacles to resource use, the sustainable use of resources must be an integral part of the Mediterranean strategy and practice of protecting the environment and ensuring the health of the people and nature for the present and future.

Invisible Voices: The Impact on Palestinian Livelihoods

Exploitation of the resources, especially natural ones, has a considerable impact on the livelihoods of the Palestinians and has been particularly harmful in the Mediterranean region. The impact of the construction/use of these resources lies in the social, economic, and ecological matters of the Palestinians, as these community members have faced displacement, loss of economic engagement, obstructions to growth, and the shutting down of traditional occupations. These consequences are a result of the utter indifference shown by the world to the Palestinians: in protecting their rights, the world chose to stay silent, and this silence allowed the plight of the Palestinians to go unaddressed. As discussions continue, the patience of the Palestinian community becomes increasingly evident. The Palestinians, like other groups, can make claims, but the lack of debate and political negotiation has perpetuated the inequity. The Palestinian community, like other communities, is entitled to make claims, but the inequity is glaring.

Shackled in the region, other resources, including life, suffer, as the loss and damage, moisture, and the quality of oxygen and other gases are astronomical. These Palestinian communities already struggle with self-sufficiency in basic and vital resources, and unlike other communities, these Palestinians lack the requisite weight. These people lack social equity and sufficiency, and this result is a consequence of resource extraction. The boundaries imposed on Palestinian waters and zones of economic exclusion have negatively impacted the desire for economic self-sufficiency and sustainable development.

Moreover, and unfortunately, the unrestricted conflict and zoning have allowed the Palestinians peace of mind and opportunities to earn. These zones are particularly offensive to the Palestinian people due to the lack of trade, lack of investment, and depletion of abundant resource capital, as they have no means to utilise natural processes for self-construction and improving their well-being. More to the point, they cannot self-muster and remain mired in over-dependency or reliance.

The impact of resource extraction on the Palestinians needs to be addressed regionally and closer to home, in agreement with the locals around the communal economic zones, and affirming their rights to land and water for economic development. We need to rapidly develop the economy in a wide and fair way, with the maximum input of the Palestinians and the rights to work and know and acquire the decisions in the development of the country and its norms. Resolving the problems in the region and among the players is possible if we manage to support the Palestinians.

International Involvement: Roles of Global Powers

The Eastern Mediterranean is of extreme importance to global powers because of the wealth of resources and its geopolitical location. Therefore, multiple global actors have been directly associated with the dynamics of resource extraction and exploration in the region. The United States, Russia, and the European Union have been identified as the predominant players with their particular interests and distinctive approaches to the Eastern Mediterranean. The United States, historically an ally of Israel, has backed the latter's activities, including offshore gas exploration and development in the region. Washington has until then been using gas to build improved diplomatic and military relations. Russia's approach is to expand in the Eastern Mediterranean by selling gas and entering regional energy partnerships. The European Union, as a group, seems to take a more balanced approach when trying to reconcile the competing interests of its members with the need to stabilise and promote cooperation in the region. More recently, the involvement of other players, such as China and Turkey, has added to the complexities of geopolitical relations.

In addition, the activities of these superpowers have shaped not only the economic and security geopolitical dimensions of the Mediterranean, but also the potential of the Palestinians to actively engage and equitably access the regional resources. Understanding the strategies and behaviours of these global players is vital for grasping the complex interplay of interests and power politics in the region. Thus, addressing the complicated intertwining of the international actors is important in formulating policies on the exclusion of Palestinians, responsible management of resources, and fostering collaboration in the region. To develop effective strategies, there is a need to understand and appreciate the complex positions of global powers to strengthen the cause for the process of recognition and inclusion of the Palestinian people and the Eastern Mediterranean stakeholders.

Toward Visibility: Advocating for Palestinian Participation

Having Palestinians involved in the management and use of resources within the region carries enormous importance for the sustenance of equity in the Mediterranean and the region of the Mediterranean as a whole. The international community constructing the case for the advocacy of the Palestinians in these matters possesses and recognises the responsibility as the stakeholder of the underlying regional resources for this particularly important issue. Failing to acknowledge the Palestinians' restrictive historical context in this case is highly discriminatory and difficult to fathom. Addressing this issue requires context. One way to achieve these goals is by utilising diplomatic tools to emphasise the significance of the region's decision-making processes related to resource management and planning. This would mean advocacy to the world and the world system organising this inclusive multinational system to appreciate the rights of the Palestinian people and integrate them into issues of negotiations, agreements, and cooperation at turnkey projects. The same ideas apply to collaboration with Palestinian authorities and organisations, which can generate early links that ensure their involvement in resource discussions for representation advocacy. Real change can only occur when individuals who adopt reasonable approaches to systemic change provide new opportunities for others to overcome their challenges. This oppression can also affect the advocacy efforts aimed at improving the region's resources. Advocacy is needed to ensure accountability and the closing of the loop in decision-making and the flow of resources. By facilitating the conditions that architects advocate for, which open the information systems and structures, Palestinian participation in supervision and decision-making can be enhanced. Within Palestinian focus communities, there exists a gap in engagement with and access to the capacity-building programs postulated for skill sets in resource education, building, and mining. To close this gap, appropriate education and support structures should be instituted to prepare Palestinians for active participation in the region's exploration, mining, and asset management. Each effort directed towards this purpose is more likely to achieve maximum impact by leveraging the appreciation that Palestinians gain from access and inclusion in these initiatives. More systemic international engagement will make it possible to configure benefit-sharing arrangements that ensure equitable and just resource extraction. Global civil society in this instance can develop and measure impact on the distributional aspects of employment creation, revenue stream distribution, and macro socio-economic growth as a unit of analysis. The more specifically these policies address the socio-economic and resource equity of Palestinians across borders, the more effectively they uphold social and international responsibility. Equally, these policies will influence the defence of productive international action. Participation from engagement to appreciating the utilitarian value of the region's issues is the measure of commitment. Consistently, this is the least effort made in the Mediterranean. What is at stake is the toll of democratic peace and social justice in the region. Political Palestinian participation is neither weak nor silenced, just currently unreciprocated for value.

11
Toward Justice
Recognition, Sovereignty, and the Path Forward

Relevant Terms of Sovereignty and Justice

Judicial and immediate exclusion of a state's self-governance is crucial for maintaining the ongoing balance of territorial dominance and jurisdictional discussions, which are complicated by the irregularities of international law and regional supremacy. Although the quest for justice serves the historical necessity of restoring balance after centuries of unfulfilled wrongs, the attainment of civility and peace remains a distant goal of the current struggle.

Observing the deep-rooted historical context of the struggle for recognition, the crux is to appreciate the complexity of justice and sovereignty in relation to the nation and its polyglot. The deep-rooted globalisation of territorial and political injustices stems from the denial of sovereignty. People often claim sovereignty but rarely achieve it, and the distinction lies in the convenience of self-governed recognition. In appreciating the evolution of recognition struggles, we underscore the essence of sovereign justice.

In addition, analysing justice and sovereignty in relation to history provides an avenue to assess the impact of such concepts in foreign relations, regional partnerships, and international law. This section will focus on key events in history and the most important points in which sovereignty has either been disputed, undermined, or strengthened, demonstrating the significant impact of such struggles on the pursuit of justice and self-determination.

In addition, the concepts of justice and sovereignty provide the foundation for the interrelationship between historical injustices and modern geopolitical relations. This section on justice and sovereignty attempts to describe the historical gaps through which the pursuit of recognition and self-government emerges, the corresponding claims and duties, and the considerable intricacies of such an effort. By analysing struggles in history, we want to explain the importance of justice and sovereignty in shaping the current geopolitical situation and creating the foundations for positive peace, stability, and prosperity.

Examining justice and sovereignty, and the recognition and territorial disputes that arise as a result, will, in the end, be critical for these communities and nations. The previously complex roots become clearer when we consider the principles of the quest for justice, as well as the gap, agency, and legitimacy that we are currently working to fulfil. This section seeks to explain the overlapping historical and current factors to construct a narrative that explains justice and sovereignty from the intricate web of global politics.

Historical Context of Recognition Struggles

The historical context, regarding withdrawn sovereignty and injustice claims, is intricate and layered with oppression, loss, and fortitude. The loss of primary identity and the current dynamics of the globe mean that the loss of self-determination and readily available statehood means that the loss of identity is central to the self-determination of the Palestinians and statehood. The fall of the Ottoman Empire and the First World War, other than the Arab Revolt, were landmark events of the early twentieth century. The fragmentation of land, coupled with the British and French mandates, ushered in a period of colonial rule that sparked dozens of wars over territory and statehood. Hopes of self-determination and freedom for the Arabs were the beginning of a century-long hostility and loss of land. The creation of the United Nations and deliberations over an independent State of Palestine and a state for the Jews integrated the complex formula of legitimacy and autonomy. Continued occupation, unchallenged settlements, and the fragmentation of land governance complicate the historical context of loss and exile.

Over the years, the pursuit of the claim for recognition has simultaneously involved diplomatic attempts, military resistance, and local support, illustrating an active attempt to exercise agency and take control of the story. International bodies and resolutions have emphasised the obligation to recognise the rights and sovereignty of the Palestinians; however, international forums have not yet provided actionable support for this recognition, and implementing a geopolitically driven power structure of support remains problematic. Recognition today is embedded in a stubborn mosaic of a sore history and unyielding persistence, and it frames the struggling discourse of justice and sovereignty. The concepts of justice and sovereignty, along with today's recognition, shape the necessary administrative discourse and the persistent need for inclusive policy suggestions that address the region's challenges.

Sovereignty and International Law

Sovereignty is one of the vital pillars of statehood, which comprises a state's power and control over its defined geographical area. For Palestine, the pursuit of self-determination and independence makes the attainment of sovereignty equally vital. International law provides the best framework to assert and defend sovereignty in the international arena. An array of legal documents, including treaties, statutes, international norms, and customs, support this goal.

One of the key bases of sovereignty in international law is the Montevideo Convention on the Rights and Duties of States from the year 1933. This important document describes the first criteria of statehood and asserts that a state must have a defined geographical territory, a settled population, a governing authority, and the ability to engage with other countries. Meeting these criteria enhances the country's claim to sovereignty because it affirms the state as a legal member of the international community.

Additionally, the principle of self-determination is of primary importance in the case of Palestinian sovereignty. One of the most important dominant rights of a person is self-determination, which under international law allows peoples to shape their own political, economic, social, and cultural systems of development. It is almost always a foundational component in achieving sovereignty, particularly in colonised and subjugated territories. The strong connection between self-determination and sovereignty provides the international legal justification needed to champion Palestinian rights and aspirations.

Furthermore, the United Nations maintains the principle of sovereignty using border determination, state recognition, international relations, and peaceful coexistence among states. The United Nations considers certain unilateral actions that violate international law, as elucidated in documents. The fundamental principle of the United Nations is the free sovereignty of its members. Military sovereignty is discussed in the General Assembly and the Security Council, where the Agency for Political and Security Affairs acts as the primary executor of international relations. The foreign relations of states considered members of military blocs receive special attention in United Nations programmes.

Justice, as exercised by international law along with doctrine and rulings on sovereignty, holds significant value in the realm of international law. The International Court of Justice is an adjudicative court that has jurisdiction over international conflicts related to borders, territory, and state sovereignty. These rights are fundamental to the constitutions of the United Nations. The outcomes of this apex court have significant consequences in international law, as its rulings are considered precedents for state matters. The bordering nations are outlined in these concepts, and the states become subjects of these international law constitutions.

The presence of law notwithstanding, the manner in which dominion and control is exercised regarding Palestine is proof on its own of the existing channels at the world's disposal to enable the people to claim their position alongside the members of the international community. Legitimate international agreements and intensive diplomatic actions aim to establish the ideal legal foundation for statehood, dominion, and self-governance.

Strategies for Diplomatic Engagement

Engaging in diplomacy is an important pillar to advocating for Palestinians in the international arena. Like other efforts, diplomacy is a multi-faceted, multi-level endeavour. On the bilateral level, it is important to work with foreign governments as primary audiences to form coalitions and alliances in support of Palestinian causes. This may include the establishment of designated diplomatic institutions like embassies and consulates to pursue conversation and negotiation with other countries. Systematic, strategic diplomatic efforts towards these countries may assist Palestinian leaders in forging strong ties within these countries and advocating for international recognition, sovereignty, and rights. In addition, these leaders may guide Palestinians to suitably utilise diplomacy, avoiding hostilities with these nations, and advocating for the Palestinian position on the international scene. Palestinians may also use international forums, international summits, and e-participation in international gatherings to pursue other diplomacy for peace efforts. Although multilateral diplomacy is also important, advocating for membership in valued international organisations like the United Nations system enables Palestinians to multiply the impact of their statehood advocacy. Through international collaboration, activism for the Palestinian right to statehood is possible. In addition to UN efforts, it includes participation in and support of regional dynamics and action coalitions on shared issues and uplift advocacy to collective action. In public diplomacy, the use of modern communication in the international arena is an important and primary consideration of the professional advocacy of Middle Eastern countries and other supporters, together with other people organising the advocacy.

These include media outreach, cultural diplomacy, public speaking, and live engagement, which serve to represent the hopes and liveliness of the Palestinians. Additionally, the use of digital diplomacy coupled with social media allows for the sharing of information and mobilisation of international support. Cultural diplomacy that involves showcasing the arts, heritage, and literature of the Palestinians enhances understanding and fosters empathy. Engaging diplomacy also includes purposeful action to negotiate and facilitate dialogue between the parties in conflict. Constructive dialogue and consensus-building processes are available with the international community through reputable mediators and conflict resolution initiatives that involve peaceable international organisations. The Palestinian leadership can integrate advocacy and multifaceted diplomacy, which includes dialogue, negotiation, and the mastery of complex international relations, to pursue justice, recognition, and sovereignty anywhere in the world.

Collaborative frameworks and alliances

These kinds of alliances are essential to support the advancement of justice, recognition, and sovereignty for the Palestinian people. Strategic international partnerships and ongoing support are essential for sustainable development. It is necessary to work with all potential stakeholders to develop these alliances, including states, intergovernmental organisations, NGOs, and civil society.

Working together with governments helps shape policies, undertake diplomacy, and advocate for the rights of the Palestinians in the global arena. Strengthening ties with the more sympathetic countries helps raise support for the Palestinians and their cause in global forums and institutions. Moreover, outreach to key intergovernmental bodies, such as the UN, the EU, and the Arab League, opens avenues for direct diplomatic initiatives, advocacy, and resource mobilisation.

This vertical and horizontal approach to advocacy support can complement the efforts of various non-governmental organisations (NGOs) in carrying out humanitarian relief activities, advocating for human rights, and empowering the voiceless and marginalised specifically for this cause. These partnerships help the organisations strengthen their advocacy and leadership on the local, regional, and global scales, as well as increase the visibility of the Palestinian cause at the international level. Also, a range of alliances with academic institutions, research and policy units, and think tanks can especially help to organise, analyse, and strategise advocacy and policy works to generate needed evidence, information, and scholarship.

Alongside this, the construction of collaborative frameworks should encompass the elements of economic empowerment and access to resources and services. Achieving self-sustainability, coupled with self-sustaining economic growth, is fundamental to supporting the Palestinian economy. Partnerships with international financial institutions, development agencies, and private sector entities can cultivate investment, entrepreneurship, and potential jobs. Investment opportunities, along with targeted collaborations, strengthen Palestinian businesses, industries, and entrepreneurs, thereby fostering economic resilience and enduring growth.

In seeking access to resources, strategic partnerships can assist in achieving the sustainable management of water, land, agriculture, and other renewable resources. Resource partnerships, coupled with regional technology transfer partnerships and environmental management, promote cross-border environmental cooperation that maintains and creates regional stability and development. This is beneficial, not only for the Palestinians but for the whole region. Moreover, partnerships with environmental and pro-green organisations highlight the region's commitment to sustainable development and the responsible management of natural resources.

In the final analysis, collaborative frameworks, along with partnerships, stand to promote the principles of justice, recognition, and sovereignty. Through collaborative efforts, a diverse array of sectors is pooled to create a single strategy that addresses the rights and aspirations of the Palestinian people, thus providing the blueprint for the region.

Economic Empowerment and Resource Access

Economic empowerment and resource access are critical to supporting the Palestinian territories' struggle for justice and autonomy. For over seventy years, Palestinians have been economically marginalised through the loss of economic opportunities and the unequal distribution of resources, which has resulted in them being reliant on external entities for aid. This issue has to be dealt with through economic development locally, but also through advocacy on access to resources. Economic development in the Palestinian territories necessitates a focus on reducing dependency and fostering self-reliance. This means there is a need for policies which will enhance the levels of entrepreneurship, innovation, and investment and deal with the relative constraints such as capital, infrastructure, and market access. In addition, the purposeful and strategic investment in the Gaza Marine and other offshore resources has the dual benefit of economic development and asserting territorial rights. Exploiting these resources with global investors in the energy market is a pertinent move towards economic self-sufficiency and autonomy.

In this case, governance of the launched development projects of these resources must be open and accountable, so the revenues obtained will positively impact the Palestinian people and their development. Furthermore, maintaining resilience of the economy by reducing dependence on the traditional economic sector of agriculture and tourism will open other new sources of economic growth. In addition, constructing supportive economy-generating infrastructure, such as transport and industrial centres, will promote economic development and improve the geographic accessibility and connection of the Palestinian territories with adjacent economies. Deliberate and active planning, together with the other carried out projects, will ensure achievement of the economically adjacent goal of recognition, self-determination and self-governance. Exerting economic pressure and utilising self-resources will increase the ability to withstand adversary externally imposed forces and also enhance the ability to self-defend and to promote and raise the Palestinian case on the world stage. This in turn will contribute towards self-determination and increasing agency and ability in the Palestinian territories. Economic empowerment and resource access are imperative for achieving self-determination and productive achievement without dependency on outside forces.

Building Institutional Foundations

Perhaps the most important undertaking is the construction of institutional frameworks, along with the pursuit of lasting peace and sovereignty. This chapter analyses the necessity of creating institutional frameworks that can support governance, law, and public administration, particularly in relation to recognition and sovereignty. This is especially challenging for the Palestinians in their pursuit of statehood. For the Palestinians, the coping mechanisms hinge on designing and building institutions that can survive external pressures and meet the needs and aspirations of the people. Such institutions can only come about through the building of a comprehensive institutional framework that combines the legislative, executive, and judicial branches. The institutions of governance, which are the pillars of governance, must incorporate the values and principles of international law and conventions. In the same vein, the institutions of governance must include, as a minimum, an independent electoral system and mechanisms for representation which are essential for the governance framework. Proportional to the governance system, its administration must incorporate regulatory bodies and control institutions. The primary function of these institutions is to control the governance system, setting norms, defining accountability, and addressing the governance and socio-economic governance gaps.

In addition to government bodies, institution-building includes the nurturing and strengthening of civil society, including civil society development, the education system, and culture. These pillars of society, civil society and culture, strengthen and deepen the pluralistic character of a Palestinian state. The facet of sustained intervention, which includes intervention on capacity building, should not be omitted. The provision of training and materials and the determination to advance the social and economic pillars of these institutions are fundamental to success. These activities will be greatly enhanced by international cooperation and assistance. Working with other nations, on the other hand, is also important. Constructing relationships with institutional builders and advancing cooperative relationships with other countries aids in the development of institutional frameworks. These efforts will help to construct essential bilateral and multilateral agreements important in the building of the state. The construction of civil and responsive institutions, on the other hand, is the construction of the state administrative system. This, at the same time, is building a community that guarantees the observance of the rule of law, civil liberties, social rights, and a truly progressive democratic polity. The construction of a Palestinian state is the construction of an internationally admired state that draws interest and impact in the contemporary global sphere. This, at the same time, is institution-building that will be the foundation of the state, which will help, over time, with flexibility and refraining from being the puppet of others in the international system.

Addressing Human Rights and Reparations

It is vital to say the answer to the problem of justice and reconciliation is 'not yet'. This is one of the many nods 'justice work' makes to the many people and communities and the many forms the suffering takes when justice remains undone. The statement acknowledges 'suffering work' as restorative to the absent and broken relations for which justice works. This sentence is the justification of the 'fifty-year' work of the Israeli-Palestinian reconciliation and justice work. The statement justifies the work to incorporate ignored legal and human injuries sustained by the Palestinian people and to make reparation for human rights violations.

Rebalancing the reconciliation efforts to address contemporary Palestinian injuries is equally, if not more, important for achieving justice. This work calls to stop ignoring, or to 'balance', the work of reconciliation for the many contemporary 'big' human rights injuries sustained by the Palestinian people. This work also calls for documentation and public acknowledgement of the human rights violations, legal and social injuries, the personal and community trauma, and the legacy of violations that continue to entrench the injustices and shape the work. This work serves as an intercession to promote a 'balanced' approach to justice and reconciliation. The goal is simply reparation. This work is directly related to the injuries suffered by the Palestinian people. This work addresses the construction of reparation law. This is very possibly the most injurious human rights work in the Palestinian case. This is why the work of reconciliation in the

Israeli community is so painful.

It is essential and displaced. This work inflicts harm and violates the right to compensation. This is the main reparation that needs to be addressed in the Palestinian people's case. This justifies nearly all human rights efforts related to reparation work within reconciliation law. This procedure is profoundly painful. 'Reconciliation work' involves reparation work, a powerful acknowledgement of the work left by reconciliation law. This incomplete work exacerbates the injuries inflicted upon Palestinian communities.

The term also includes the reparation for human rights laws injured by the state of Israel. This situation is deeply painful and largely overlooked. This acknowledgement needs to be added to reparations laws centred on human rights.

It profoundly injures and ignores reparation work at the heart of the law. It also harms and significantly overlooks reconciliation law, which aims to promote both reparation and reconciliation through the development of laws. It needs to be addressed. The situation is deeply painful.

Additionally, to achieve reparations and respond to violations of human rights, one must also hold accountable those who commit, enable, or deny violations. Holding such individuals accountable is a means of achieving justice for the victims and preventing similar violations in the future. This process is inescapably a function of the willingness to enforce the spirit of the relevant international legal instruments and ensure that those who perpetrate or condone violations of human rights are made to answer for their misconduct.

Of course, the determination of reparations must take into account other aspects. This is primarily the provision of concrete responses to the victims of partial or full human rights violations. These responses include compensation, restitution, rehabilitation, and satisfaction. Reparations are designed to respond to the economic and emotional damages inflicted onto victims and, in the process, recognise their worth and attempt to restore their justice.

One of the most important aspects of addressing human rights and implementing reparations is the incorporation of individuals and communities impacted into the decision process. Involvement of communities directly impacted ensures that reparative actions taken are appropriate to their lived experiences and needs, and action directly impacting individuals and communities fosters acquired agency and empowerment. In addition, the engagement of civil society organisations, human rights advocates, and transnational actors of civil societies, advocacy networks, and human rights organisations may considerably assist the advocacy for reparations and the incorporation of the marginalised voices, civil society transnational networks, advocacy frameworks, and organisations to echo the marginalised voices of communities and consolidate them.

There are lessons to be learnt from the international community and global advocacy structures. Advocating for driven frameworks, action plans, and approaches to reparations should draw on the advocacy for civil society networks focused on the right to reparations for human rights violations. Assessing civil action and its interface for reparations, including transitional justice, truth and reconciliation commissions, and international jurisprudence, holds significant value. The strategies of other conflict-affected societies, particularly in the Israeli-Palestinian context, may be most influenced by the advocacy for reparative justice through internationally accepted networks that support the right to reparations within dependent international frameworks.

The pursuit of redress and reparations for human rights violations addresses the need to correct historical wrongs and helps signal the possibility of a more equitable and inclusive future. It demands a commitment to facing the challenging realities of the situation, the need for accountability and redress, and the prioritisation of the needs of those whose lives have been most deeply affected by the violence. Human rights violations and the need for reparations within the hierarchy of the goals for justice and reconciliation are key to the roadmap for enduring peace and dignity for all.

Case Studies: Global Precedents

As part of finding possible avenues to accomplish justice and self-determination for the Palestinian people, it would be beneficial to look into global case studies regarding such matters. One of the most striking ones to investigate would be the case of South Africa and what it underwent after the abolishment of apartheid. The post-apartheid South Africa Truth and Reconciliation Commission expounds profound understandings concerning the intricacies of dealing with the aftermath of historical injustices and the possible sustainable frameworks for peace. In attempting to understand the frameworks of addressing human rights violations and the attempts to extend reparations, the situation of the Palestinians can be illuminated, and possible constructive and unconstructive methods can be garnered. Another interesting case is the conflict resolution of Northern Ireland through the 1998 Good Friday Agreement, which was a watershed moment in the history of Ireland regarding the peace process and self-determination. It is beneficial to analyse the evolution of the negotiations, the implementation of power-sharing policies, and the establishment of multi-community governance to yield a plethora of insights intended for the Palestinian case regarding sovereignty and statehood aspirations. Other insights include the attempts at reconciliation and transitional justice in post-conflict Colombia and Rwanda, which serve as a basis for post-explanation of the synthesis of different perspectives and attempts at justice for past injustices.

The scenarios bring out the critical fusion between multiple legal aspects, politics, and social reconciliation in deciding the constructive way out in terms of justice and sovereignty. The case studies and documents of the world provide the Palestinian struggle with specific refinements needed for its journey toward self-determination and lasting peace.

Vision for a Sustainable Peace Process

Within the context of the Israeli-Palestinian conflict, the complex means of achieving a sustainable peace process requires the formulation of a comprehensive, multifaceted, and integrative approach to deal with the specifics of the situation at hand. The vision of a sustainable peace process, drawing on international best practices and lessons, must include a number of interrelated elements. First, it requires mutual recognition and respect for the sovereignty and self-determination of both the Palestinian State and Israel after ending the military occupation, and withdrawing from illegal settlements. This recognition and respect serve as the bedrock of any enduring resolution. Further, there must be a transparent and responsible approach to the equitable distribution of resources, infrastructure, and economic opportunities accessible to the Palestinians, given the fact that they are those who suffer the horrors of the Israeli occupation. Addressing these issues of socio-economic justice as well as the reconciliation of, and with, the past through truth and recognition of past wrongdoings is essential for peace to hold. Such an approach is informed by peace-building practices around the globe that incorporate transitional justice, reparation, and the restoration of dignity to all survivors of conflicts. In addition, there is a need for the direct involvement and commitment of the surrounding and even international key stakeholders that wish to promote stability and collaboration for the realisation of the two-state solution to the conflict, which in turn enhances the process of peace on a global scale.

The participation of the international community, including neighbouring countries, powerful states, and international organisations, is crucial in the provision of sustained diplomacy and development support for the peace process. A peace process extends to the creation of peaceful and democratic societies. This forward-looking vision embraces the democratic and inclusive participation of all the Palestinians (including those who resisted with arms against the occupation of their country) in self-governing institutions that enable them to take part in the governance of their communities and their interests to ensure making decisions together for all that concerns their national interests. The process expands the participation to inclusiveness and the richer diversity of the margin of society to close the gaps, build the bridge, cross the bridge of intercultural dialogue, and cultivate common ownership of peaceful coexistence. The education for sustainable development empowers future generations for peace and development, embracing a long-term engagement and commitment to dialogue in the process that is sustainable on education and a culture of future generations. This vision embraces a sustainable and inclusive peace process that is free and democratic, which means that no Palestinian faction should be excluded whether it is affiliated or not to the PLO. The picture that is sketched is one that embodies justice, equality, and dignity. It is a vision that responds to one of the lasting and unresolved challenges of the contemporary world. By invoking a sustainable peace process, these transformative principles and sources of integration seek to stabilise the region.